The New Classic **Cook**

GOODFOODFAST

lose weight – feel great

Time Inc.
HOME ENTERTAINMENT

Good Food Fast: lose weight, feel great.
First published by ACP Magazines Ltd 2001

Food editor Pamela Clark
Photographer Andre Martin
Stylist Sarah O'Brien

Managing Editor Susan Tomnay
Publisher Sue Wannan

Time Inc.
HOME ENTERTAINMENT

Publisher Richard Fraiman
Executive Director, Marketing Services Carol Pittard
Director, Retail & Special Sales Tom Mifsud
Marketing Director, Branded Businesses Swati Rao
Director, New Product Development Peter Harper
Assistant Financial Director Steven Sandonato
Prepress Manager Emily Rabin
Product Manager Victoria Alfonso
Associate Book Production Manager Suzanne Janso
Associate Prepress Manager Anne-Michelle Gallero

special thanks:
Bozena Bannett, Alexandra Bliss, Glenn Buonocore,
Bernadette Corbie, Robert Marasco, Brooke McGuire,
Jonathan Polsky, Ilene Schreider, Adriana Tierno

Cover and interior design by Anne-Michelle Gallero

ISBN: 1-932994-29-7

We welcome your comments and suggestions about Time Inc.
Home Entertainment. Please write to us at:
Time Inc. Home Entertainment,
Attention: Book Editors,
P.O. Box 11016, Des Moines, IA 50336-1016.

If you would like to order any of our hardcover
Collector's Edition books, please call us at 1-800-327-6388.
(Monday through Friday, 7:00 a.m.– 8:00 p.m.
or Saturday, 7:00 a.m.– 6:00 p.m. Central Time).

TABLE OF CONTENTS

4   INCIDENTAL EXERCISE

6   BREAKFAST

28   DIPPING IN

30   LIGHT MEALS

62   NIBBLES

64   MAINS

104   SNACKS

106   DESSERTS

124   GLOSSARY

128   MAKE YOUR OWN STOCK

INCIDENTAL EXERCISE

We all know that exercise is good for us. It makes us feel good, reduces the risk of heart disease, lowers blood pressure, helps control weight, improves posture and helps to prevent osteoporosis. Yet many of us still don't exercise. Why not?

Perhaps we can't bear the thought of going to a gym with all those tanned and toned bodies; perhaps there's never time for a regular walk around the park; or perhaps, despite our best intentions, we just don't enjoy it enough to maintain an exercise regimen. Well, here's the good news: You're probably doing more exercise than you think, just going about your daily life – and with very little effort, it's possible to do a whole lot more! This isn't a formal exercise routine, but a series of tips on how to increase your daily level of activity by making a few minor changes to your usual habits.

AT HOME

>> See **household chores** as an opportunity to burn a few calories rather than just drudgery. Put on some upbeat music and dust or sweep in time to the beat.

>> When there's time, **mix ingredients by hand** instead of using a mixer – it will take longer but it's wonderful for hand and arm strength and for relieving stress and frustration.

>> Instead of setting the table all at once, **walk around the table** placing the forks, then around again placing the knives, and so forth.

>> Don't use your dryer (unless it's raining, of course) – **hang your laundry out** on the line in the fresh air, bending and stretching with each item.

>> **When watching television**, don't just sit there: circle your feet or jiggle your arms and legs. Don't use the remote control: get up and change the channel or adjust the volume. During commercials, walk to the other end of the room or get up and stretch a few times.

>> Instead of inviting a friend for coffee, suggest that you **meet in a nearby park and go for a stroll** while catching up on the latest gossip.

SHOPPING

>> Instead of repeatedly circling the parking lot looking for that perfect spot, **park farther away and walk the extra distance** - you'll probably get to the stores faster anyway.

>> Always **walk your shopping cart back to the store** instead of leaving it in the parking lot.

>> **Use the stairs** rather than elevators or escalators. If you can't find the stairs, walk up the escalator instead of just standing still for the ride.

>> In the supermarket, to help keep your arms toned, gently **push and pull your cart backwards** and **forwards** while walking down the aisles. You can also do this while waiting in the checkout line.

IN THE CAR

>> **Turn on the radio** and tap your hands or bop along to the music.

>> If you drive an automatic car, instead of letting your left leg go to sleep during the trip, **tap your foot in time to the music** or circle your foot in each direction to stimulate circulation.

>> Train yourself to see a red traffic light as the perfect opportunity to work out a muscle or two - try pelvic floor exercises, or **pushing and pulling on the steering wheel, or** squeezing and releasing the wheel with your hands.

AT WORK

>> **Get off the bus or train one stop earlier** on the way to and from work.

>> **Get out of the elevator one floor below your office and use the stairs.** As you grow fitter you can gradually increase the number of flights of stairs.

>> Leave some walking shoes at work and **take a walk during your lunch break.**

>> **Go window-shopping** - it doesn't cost anything to look and will use up calories as well as get you out of the office.

>> **Walk farther than your usual sandwich shop** and find a different place to eat.

>> **Place your trash can away from your desk and get up and walk to it** when needed - resisting the urge to improve your aim!

FIT WITHOUT A FUSS

In the past it was thought that you had to exercise vigorously for a minimum of 30 minutes three to four times a week to get any benefits. However, this is not the case. Short duration activity, approximately 10 minutes each, that adds up to 30 minutes a day has been shown to help in decreasing blood pressure, blood cholesterol and body weight. This 30 minutes of accumulated exercise does not have to be vigorous, just at a level where your breathing is a little heavier than usual. And it doesn't need to involve joggers and bicycle pants - for instance, 30 minutes of gentle activity, such as sweeping the floor or gardening, will use up to 85 calories. If you did this daily, it would add up to 30,000 calories a year, which is the equivalent of 10 pounds of fat! Get out that broom...

BREAKFAST

From flavor- and vitamin-packed juice combos to more substantial hot dishes, this selection of breakfast recipes will make the most important meal of the day also one of the most enjoyable.

buckwheat pancakes with caramelized banana

 preparation time 10 minutes (plus refrigeration time) • cooking time 20 minutes

1/4	cup self-rising flour
1/4	cup buckwheat flour
1 1/2	tablespoons sugar
1/4	teaspoon ground cinnamon
1	egg
3/4	cup skim milk
1 1/2	tablespoons butter
1/4	cup firmly packed brown sugar
4	medium bananas (about 1 3/4 pounds), sliced thickly
3	tablespoons water

The seeds of the buckwheat plant are ground into the flour that is the essential ingredient in Japanese soba, Russian blini and delicious pancakes such as these.

SERVES 4

per serving 6.1g fat; 307 calories

serving suggestion
These pancakes also make a lovely dessert.

tips Fresh strawberries may be used as a filling instead of caramelized bananas. Dust pancakes with powdered sugar before serving.

1 Combine flours, sugar and cinnamon in medium bowl; gradually whisk in combined egg and milk until smooth. Cover; refrigerate 30 minutes.

2 Meanwhile, melt butter in large skillet; add brown sugar and cook, stirring, until dissolved. Add banana and the water; cook, uncovered, stirring occasionally, about 2 minutes or until banana is caramelized.

3 Pour 1/4 cup batter into heated, 8-inch non-stick skillet; cook pancake until browned on both sides. Repeat with remaining batter to make four pancakes. Cover to keep warm.

4 Just before serving, halve each pancake; divide halves among serving plates. Spoon banana mixture onto each half; fold to enclose filling, drizzle with caramel.

fruit salad with honey yogurt

 preparation time 15 minutes

3/4	cup low-fat yogurt
3	tablespoons honey
7	ounces peeled, coarsely chopped pineapple
7	ounces seeded, peeled, coarsely chopped cantaloupe
8	ounces strawberries, halved
8	ounces blueberries
1	large banana, sliced thinly
3	tablespoons passion fruit pulp
2	teaspoons lime juice
12	fresh mint leaves

We have the Greeks to thank for the serendipitous combination of yogurt and honey, and the benevolence of the tropics for the combination of fruits. You need only small quantities of pineapple and cantaloupe for this recipe, so buy the smallest ones you can find. Two passion fruit will supply the right amount of pulp.

1 Combine yogurt and honey in small bowl.

2 Just before serving, combine remaining ingredients in large bowl; serve with honey yogurt.

SERVES 4

per serving 2g fat; 179 calories

tips Lime juice not only adds flavor to this recipe but also prevents the banana from discoloring.
Honey yogurt can be made a day ahead; store, covered, in refrigerator.

pineapple and mint frappé

 preparation time 20 minutes

1	large pineapple (about 4 pounds), peeled, chopped coarsely
40	ice cubes, crushed
1 1/2	tablespoons finely chopped fresh mint

The word frappé is a French description for frozen or chilled drinks and dishes.

1 Blend or process pineapple until smooth; transfer to large pitcher.

2 Stir in ice and mint; pour into serving glasses.

SERVES 4
(makes 6 cups)

per 1 1/2-cup serving
0.3g fat; 99 calories

 tips Pineapple can be processed several hours ahead. Cover; refrigerate until ready to combine with ice and serve. You can crush the ice in a blender or food processor.

citrus compote

 preparation time 20 minutes (plus standing time)

2	large limes
3	large oranges
	(about 2 pounds)
2	medium pink grapefruit
	(about 1 3/4 pounds)
2	teaspoons sugar
1/2	vanilla bean, split
1 1/2	tablespoons small fresh
	mint leaves

SERVES 4

per serving
0.7g fat; 164 calories

1 Grate the peel of 1 lime and 1 orange finely; reserve grated peel. Peel remaining lime, remaining oranges, and grapefruit.

2 Segment all citrus over a large bowl to save juice, removing and discarding pith from each segment. Add segments to bowl with sugar, vanilla bean and reserved grated peel; stir gently to combine.

3 Let stand, covered, at room temperature 5 minutes; sprinkle with mint leaves.

fresh berry frappé

 preparation time 10 minutes

10	ounces blueberries
8	ounces raspberries
40	ice cubes, crushed
1/2	cup fresh orange juice

You can also use frozen berries for this recipe. Experiment with other berries-strawberries, blackberries, boysenberries-and adjust combinations to your taste.

1 Blend or process berries until just smooth. Push berry puree through a fine sieve into large bowl; discard solids in sieve.

2 Stir in ice and juice; spoon into serving glasses.

SERVES 4
(makes 3 1/2 cups)

per serving 0.4g fat; 70 calories

tip Depending on the sweetness of the berries, you may need to add sugar. You can crush the ice in a blender or food processor.

mushroom and parsley omelet

 preparation time 10 minutes
cooking time 10 minutes

4	eggs, beaten lightly
6	egg whites
1	pound cremini mushrooms, sliced thinly
1/3	cup loosely packed, coarsely chopped fresh flat-leaf parsley

1 Whisk beaten egg with egg whites in medium bowl.

2 Cook mushrooms in heated, 8-inch non-stick skillet, stirring, until tender. Place mushrooms with parsley in small bowl.

3 Return pan to stove, add a quarter of the egg mixture; cook, tilting pan, over medium heat until almost set. Place a quarter of the mushroom mixture evenly over half of the omelet; fold omelet over to enclose filling, slide onto serving plate.

4 Repeat with remaining egg and mushroom mixtures to make four omelets in total.

SERVES 4

per serving
5.6g fat; 126 calories

serving suggestions
Serve with thick slices of toasted sourdough bread.

tip Basil can be substituted for parsley.

breakfast for four

 preparation time 10 minutes · cooking time 25 minutes

2	large plum tomatoes, quartered
4	eggs
4	slices multi-grain bread
2	ounces lean ham
2	cups baby spinach

SERVES 4

per serving 7g fat; 160 calories

1 Preheat oven to 425. Line baking sheet with parchment paper.

2 Place tomatoes, cut-side up, on prepared baking sheet; roast, uncovered, about 25 minutes or until softened and lightly browned.

3 Meanwhile, place enough water in a large, shallow non-stick skillet to come halfway up the sides; bring to a boil. Crack eggs, one at a time, into small bowl, sliding each into pan; allow water to return to a boil. Cover pan, turn off heat; let stand about 4 minutes or until a light film of egg white has set over each yolk.

4 Toast bread slices until lightly browned on both sides.

5 Using a slotted spoon, carefully remove eggs, one at a time, from skillet; place egg, still on spoon, on paper towel-lined plate to blot up any poaching liquid. Serve toast topped with ham, spinach, egg then tomato.

banana smoothie

 preparation time 5 minutes

2	cups skim milk
2	medium bananas, chopped coarsely
1/2	cup low-fat yogurt
1 1/2	tablespoons honey
1 1/2	tablespoons wheat germ
1/4	teaspoon ground cinnamon

A health-food craze that began in San Francisco in the 1980s still has blenders working overtime around the world.

1 Blend or process ingredients until smooth. Serve immediately.

SERVES 4
(makes 1 quart)
per 1-cup serving 0.9g fat; 151 calories

tip Use frozen bananas or add ice cubes to the blender for a thicker smoothie.

oatmeal with apple compote

 preparation time 10 minutes • cooking time 10 minutes

2	medium apples
1/4	cup sugar
1/4	teaspoon ground cinnamon
1/4	cup water
8	dried apricots
1 1/2	tablespoons golden raisins
1	cup rolled oats
1	cup skim milk
1 1/2	cups boiling water
3	tablespoons brown sugar

There can be few things as comforting or nutritious as a warming bowl of oatmeal. Here, it's given a natural flavor enhancer with the addition of gently cooked cinnamon-spiced apples.

1 Peel, core and slice apples thickly; combine apples with sugar, cinnamon and the water in medium pot. Cook, stirring, over low heat until sugar dissolves. Bring to a boil, reduce heat; simmer, uncovered, 5 minutes. Add apricots and raisins; simmer, uncovered, about 5 minutes or until apple is tender.

2 Meanwhile, combine oats, milk and the boiling water in another medium pot; return to a boil. Reduce heat; simmer, uncovered, about 5 minutes or until mixture thickens.

3 Serve oatmeal with apple compote, sprinkled with brown sugar.

SERVES 4

per serving 2.1g fat; 244 calories

tip Any other dried fruit, such as prunes, pears or peaches, could be used instead of the apricots.

grilled mango and ricotta with english muffins

 preparation time 10 minutes · cooking time 5 minutes

1 cup low-fat ricotta cheese

3/4 cup low-fat tropical-fruit flavored yogurt (such as pineapple, mango, or kiwi)

2 small mangoes (about 1 1/3 pounds)

2 white english muffins

3 tablespoons passion fruit pulp

You need two passion fruit to get the pulp for this recipe.

SERVES 4

per serving
5.2g fat; 246 calories

serving suggestion
Drizzle some maple syrup over the mangoes, if extra sweetness is desired.

tip If mangoes are unavailable, you can substitute sliced fresh pineapple.

1 Whisk cheese and yogurt together in medium bowl until mixture is smooth.

2 Halve mangoes, discarding pits; remove skin, cut each half in half.

3 Cook mango on heated oiled grill or grill pan until browned on both sides.

4 Just before serving, split muffins; toast on both sides. Place half a muffin on each serving plate; top with cheese mixture and mango, drizzle with passion fruit pulp.

JUICES

If you don't own a juicer, blend or process the fruit for these drinks until pureed, then push the mixture through a fine sieve into a large pitcher.

grapefruit passion

preparation time 10 minutes

Give a cold a healthy blast of vitamin C with this drink. Originating in Brazil, the passion fruit was named by Jesuit priests for the appearance of the flower, which brought to mind the crucifixion and the crown of thorns. You need about 24 passion fruit to get 2 cups of pulp.

4	medium ruby grapefruit (about 3 3/4 pounds), peeled, chopped coarsely
10	ounces raspberries
2	cups passion fruit pulp
1	teaspoon sugar

1. Push fruit through juicer. Add sugar; stir to combine.

SERVES 4
(makes 1 quart)

per 1-cup serving 1.2g fat; 201 calories

tip You can use oranges or tangerines instead of grapefruit, if you prefer a sweeter juice.

vegetable juice

preparation time 10 minutes

2	medium beets (about 1 1/3 pounds), trimmed, quartered
3	trimmed celery stalks
4	large carrots, halved lengthwise
2	small apples, quartered
2	medium oranges, peeled, quartered

1. Push ingredients through juicer. Stir to combine.

SERVES 4
(makes 1 quart)

per 1-cup serving 0.4g fat; 139 calories

tip For a more tart drink, you could use one large grapefruit (about 1 pound) instead of the oranges.

tropical delight

preparation time 10 minutes

You need about 14 ounces of peeled and chopped pineapple for this recipe.

1	small pineapple (1 3/4 pounds), peeled, chopped coarsely
4	medium apples (1 1/3 pounds), chopped coarsely
2	medium oranges, peeled, chopped coarsely

1. Push fruit through juicer. Stir to combine.

SERVES 4
(makes 1 quart)

per 1-cup serving 0.3g fat; 122 calories

melon mania

preparation time 10 minutes

Capture the essence of summer with this refreshing combination. You need a section of watermelon weighing about 3 1/3 pounds and half of both a medium cantaloupe and a honeydew melon for this recipe

1 1/3	pounds seeded, peeled, coarsely chopped cantaloupe
1 1/3	pounds seeded, peeled, coarsely chopped honeydew melon
2 1/4	pounds seeded, peeled, coarsely chopped watermelon
8	ounces strawberries, halved

1. Push fruit through juicer. Stir to combine.

SERVES 4
(makes 1 quart)

per 1-cup serving 1.1g fat; 144 calories

tip Refrigerate the fruit before processing so that the flavors are at their fullest.

low-fat toasted muesli

 preparation time 10 minutes · cooking time 30 minutes (plus standing time)

2	cups rolled oats
1	cup triticale flakes
1	cup unprocessed bran
1	cup barley flakes
1	cup soy whole-wheat flakes
1/2	cup rice flakes
1/2	cup rye flakes
1/4	cup macadamia oil
1/2	cup honey
1/3	cup pumpkin seeds
3	tablespoons flax seeds
3	tablespoons sunflower seeds
1	cup coarsely chopped dried apricots
1	cup coarsely chopped dried apples
1	cup seeded, coarsely chopped dried dates
1	cup golden raisins

The word muesli translates from German as mixture, liberally interpreted by the Swiss as a wholesome flavor-packed combination of cereals, nuts, fruit, and honey or sugar.

MAKES 12 cups

per 1/2-cup serving
7.2g fat; 232 calories

serving suggestion
Serve with skim milk and peaches, nectarines or berries.

 tip · Store in airtight container in refrigerator for up to 3 months.

1 Preheat oven to 350.

2 Combine cereals, oil and honey in large shallow baking pan; toast, uncovered, about 30 minutes or until browned lightly, stirring at least three times during cooking time. Let toasted cereal cool 10 minutes, then stir in remaining ingredients.

tropical fruit lassi

 preparation time 15 minutes

1	cup low-fat yogurt
1/2	cup water
3	ounces seeded, peeled, coarsely chopped cantaloupe
3	ounces peeled, coarsely chopped pineapple
1	small mango, peeled, chopped coarsely
3	ounces strawberries, halved
1 1/2	tablespoons sugar
6	ice cubes

The lassi is a frothy yogurt or buttermilk drink that has migrated into many cuisines from its home country, India. You need only 3 ounces each of peeled and chopped pineapple and cantaloupe for this recipe, so buy the smallest ones you can find – and eat what's left as part of a fruit salad later.

1 Blend or process ingredients until smooth. Serve immediately.

SERVES 4
(makes 1 quart)

per 1-cup serving
1.4g fat; 117 calories

tip Vary the fruit according to the season and your preferences.

day-before muffins

 preparation time 15 minutes (plus refrigeration time) · cooking time 30 minutes

2/3	cup coarsely chopped dried apricots
1/2	cup coarsely chopped dried figs
1 1/3	cups bran-flakes break fast cereal
1 1/2	cups skim milk
1 1/4	cups firmly packed brown sugar
2	tablespoons honey
1 1/4	cups self-rising flour
1/2	cup pecans, chopped coarsely

1 Combine apricots, figs, cereal, milk, sugar and honey in large bowl; mix well. Cover; refrigerate overnight.

2 Preheat oven to 400. Lightly grease four holes of a six-hole oversize (Texas) muffin pan.

3 Stir flour and nuts into apricot mixture. Spoon mixture into prepared muffin pan; bake about 30 minutes. Serve muffins hot or cold.

SERVES 4

per serving 11.1g fat; 469 calories

serving suggestion Serve with fresh fruit preserves or top with dried apricots; dust with powdered sugar, if desired.

 tip Muffins can be frozen for up to 2 months.

When you have overnight guests or friends coming for breakfast, prepare ahead for a breakfast of muffins fresh from the oven! The muffin batter is partially made the day before and refrigerated overnight, needing only a few more minutes of preparation before baking and serving. We used All Bran for the breakfast cereal.

hash browns with ham and cherry tomatoes

 preparation time 15 minutes • cooking time 25 minutes

7	ounces shredded lean ham
4	large potatoes (about 2 1/2 pounds), grated coarsely
1	egg white, beaten lightly
1	cooking-oil spray
7	ounces cherry tomatoes
2	scallions, trimmed, chopped coarsely

SERVES 4

per serving
2.9g fat; 268 calories

tip Wilted baby spinach leaves can also be served with these hash browns.

1 Preheat oven to 425.

2 Place ham on baking pan; cook, uncovered, until browned lightly.

3 Meanwhile, combine potatoes and egg white in large bowl; divide into four portions. Spray heated large non-stick skillet with cooking-oil spray; cook one portion of potato mixture, forming into flat pancake shape while cooking, until browned on both sides and cooked through. Repeat with remaining portions. Cover patties to keep warm.

4 Cook tomatoes in same pan until just beginning to soften. Serve hash browns topped with ham, tomatoes and scallions.

DIPPING IN

Indulge yourself with this collection of figure-friendly dips, served with plain crackers, toasted flat bread or oven-baked bagel chips.

herb ricotta dip

preparation time 15 minutes

3	tablespoons skim milk
5	ounces packaged low-fat cream cheese
3	ounces low-fat ricotta cheese
2	cloves garlic, quartered
2	teaspoons lemon juice
1 1/2	tablespoons coarsely chopped fresh chives
1 1/2	tablespoons coarsely chopped fresh flat-leaf parsley
1 1/2	tablespoons coarsely chopped fresh thyme leaves
1 1/2	tablespoons coarsely chopped capers

1. Blend or process milk, cheeses, garlic and juice until smooth.

2. Stir in herbs and capers.

MAKES 1 1/4 CUPS

per 1 1/2 tablespoons 2.3g fat; 30 calories

serving suggestion Serve with vegetable sticks, crackers, or thinly sliced toasted baguette.

tips Dip can be made 3 hours ahead of time and refrigerated, covered. Alternatively, make cheese mixture the day before and stir in herbs just before serving.

tomato salsa

preparation time 15 minutes

3	medium tomatoes (about 1 1/4 pounds), seeded, chopped finely
1	small avocado, chopped finely
1	medium red onion, chopped finely
2	red serrano or Thai chiles, seeded, chopped finely
3	tablespoons coarsely chopped fresh cilantro leaves
4	ounces canned corn, rinsed, drained
1 1/2	tablespoons lemon juice

1. Combine ingredients in medium bowl.

MAKES 2 CUPS

per 1 1/2 tablespoons 1.4g fat; 19 calories
serving suggestion Serve with baked tortilla
corn chips or toasted flour tortilla wedges.

sweet chili dip

preparation time 5 minutes

8	ounces softened packaged low-fat cream cheese
1/4	cup mild sweet Thai chili sauce
1 1/2	tablespoons coarsely chopped fresh cilantro leaves

1. Combine ingredients in small bowl; mix well.

MAKES 1 1/4 CUPS

per 1 1/2 tablespoons 2.9g fat; 37 calories
serving suggestion
Serve with crackers or vegetable sticks.

LIGHT MEALS

Whether you want a quick lunch or a light supper – or just to keep the munchies at bay in between – this appealing selection of low-fat soups, sandwiches, stir-fries and salads should keep you satisfied.

vegetable and red lentil soup

preparation time 5 minutes • cooking time 25 minutes

3	tablespoons mild curry paste
14	-ounce can crushed tomatoes, undrained
3	cups chicken stock
2	large carrots, chopped finely
2	trimmed celery stalks, chopped finely
1	medium potato, chopped finely
1	large zucchini, chopped finely
3/4	cup red lentils
1/2	cup frozen peas
1/3	cup light coconut milk
3	tablespoons coarsely chopped fresh cilantro leaves

Used since prehistoric times, lentils are an excellent source of protein, fiber and B vitamins. As the Hindu proverb says: "Rice is good, but lentils are my life."

SERVES 6

per serving 4.4g fat; 167 calories

serving suggestion
Accompany with Indian bread and a small bowl of raita (finely chopped cucumber combined with low-fat yogurt).

 tip A hotter curry paste or some finely chopped fresh chile can be added to intensify the flavor.

1 Cook curry paste in heated large pot, stirring, about 1 minute or until fragrant. Add tomatoes, stock, carrots, celery, potato and zucchini; bring to a boil. Reduce heat; simmer, covered, 5 minutes.

2 Add lentils to soup mixture; return to a boil. Reduce heat; simmer, uncovered, about 10 minutes or until lentils are just tender. Add peas; return to a boil. Reduce heat; simmer, uncovered, until peas are just tender.

3 Remove soup from heat; stir in remaining ingredients.

chicken broth with rice noodles

 preparation time 15 minutes • cooking time 25 minutes (plus cooling time)

6	cups chicken stock
2	cups water
4	-inch piece fresh ginger, sliced thinly
12	ounces boneless, skinless chicken breasts
1	pound fresh rice noodles
1/4	cup lime juice
1 1/2	tablespoons fish sauce
4	scallions, chopped coarsely
2	red serrano or Thai chiles, seeded, sliced thinly
3	tablespoons coarsely chopped fresh cilantro leaves
1	cup bean sprouts

You'll find a version of this popular soup in most Asian cuisine; this one has a Thai accent.

1 Bring stock, water and ginger to a boil in large pot. Add chicken, return to a boil, reduce heat; simmer, covered, about 15 minutes or until chicken is cooked through. Remove chicken; cool 10 minutes then shred coarsely.

2 Return broth mixture to a boil; add noodles, juice and sauce. Reduce heat; simmer, stirring, until noodles are just tender.

3 Add chicken and remaining ingredients to broth; stir over medium heat until hot.

SERVES 4

per serving 7.4g fat; 409 calories

serving suggestion Serve with wedges of lime and follow with a selection of tropical fruit.

 tips Coarsely chopped leafy green Chinese vegetables, such as bok choy or water spinach, can be added to this broth.
Dried rice noodles, or the thicker rice stick noodles, can be substituted for fresh noodles; they need to be soaked in boiling water for about 5 minutes and drained before being added to the stock.

pea and potato soup

preparation time 10 minutes
• cooking time 30 minutes
(plus cooling time)

3   cups chicken stock
2   medium leeks
    (about 1 1/2 pounds),
    sliced thinly
1   clove garlic,
    crushed
2   medium potatoes,
    chopped coarsely
4   cups (1 pound)
    frozen peas
3   cups water
3   tablespoons finely
    shredded fresh
    mint leaves

Leek and potato are natural allies
when teamed in this satisfying
winter soup. Take care to wash
the leeks well under cold water to
remove any grit.

1   Heat 3 tablespoons of the
    stock in large pot, add leek
    and garlic; cook, stirring, about
    10 minutes or until leek is soft.

2   Add remaining stock, pota-
    toes, peas and the water to
    pan; bring to a boil. Reduce
    heat; simmer, covered, about
    15 minutes or until vegetables
    are tender. Cool 10 minutes.

3   Blend or process soup, in
    batches, until smooth.

4   Return soup to same cleaned
    pan; stir over medium heat
    until hot. Stir in mint just
    before serving.

SERVES 4

per serving
1.8g fat; 197 calories

serving suggestion
Herb rolls or biscuits would make a
good accompaniment for this soup.

beef and noodle stir-fry

 preparation time 15 minutes (plus soaking time) • cooking time 20 minutes

8	ounces rice stick noodles
2	teaspoons peanut oil
1	pound beef tenderloin steaks, sliced thinly
1	clove garlic, crushed
1 1/2	tablespoons finely chopped lemongrass
2	red serrano or Thai chiles, seeded, sliced thinly
1/3	cup lime juice
1 1/2	tablespoons fish sauce
2	cups baby arugula leaves
1	cup bean sprouts
1/2	cup loosely packed fresh cilantro leaves
1/2	cup loosely packed fresh mint leaves
3	scallions, sliced thinly
1	small cucumber, seeded, sliced thinly

Rice stick noodles, also known as sen lek (Thai) and ho fun (Chinese), are wide, flat noodles made from rice flour. They must be softened by being soaked in boiling water before use.

SERVES 4
per serving
9.5g fat; 367 calories
serving suggestion
Serve with wedges of lime and a bowl of finely chopped fresh chile so that diners can adjust flavors according to their tastes.

tips You can substitute baby spinach leaves or watercress for the arugula.
Lemongrass can be found in most Asian supermarkets; buy it fresh, rather than frozen or dried. You can also substitute grated lemon peel; the peel of one lemon is equivalent to two lemongrass stalks.

1 Place noodles in large heatproof bowl, cover with boiling water; let stand 5 minutes or until tender, drain.

2 Heat half of the oil in wok or large skillet; cook beef, in batches, until browned.

3 Heat remaining oil in wok; cook garlic, lemongrass and chiles until fragrant. Return beef to wok with juice and sauce, stir-fry until heated through. Add noodles, stir-fry until combined. Stir in remaining ingredients; serve immediately.

steak sandwich

preparation time 15 minutes • cooking time 15 minutes

2	small leeks, sliced thinly
1 1/2	tablespoons brown sugar
1/4	cup dry white wine
1 1/2	tablespoons whole-grain mustard
2	medium zucchini, sliced thinly
2	baby eggplants, sliced thinly
2	medium tomatoes, sliced thickly
4	3-ounce fillet mignon steaks
8	slices thick white bread
1	cup mesclun salad greens

Mesclun is a mixture of various baby salad greens; substitute any single lettuce variety if you prefer.

1 Cook leeks, with about 3 tablespoons of water to prevent sticking, in medium non-stick skillet over low heat, stirring, until softened. Add sugar, wine and mustard; cook, stirring, about 10 minutes or until leek is browned and liquid evaporates.

2 Meanwhile, cook zucchini, eggplant and tomato on oiled grill or grill pan until vegetables are browned all over and just tender. Keep warm.

3 Cook beef on heated oiled grill or grill pan until browned on both sides and cooked as desired.

4 Toast bread lightly. Sandwich each steak, with a quarter each of the vegetables and mesclun, between two pieces of toast.

SERVES 4

per serving   8g fat; 528 calories

serving suggestion   Serve with oven-baked potato wedges.

 tips   Leeks may be cooked longer to caramelize them, if you prefer. For a cheaper cut of steak, use boneless beef sirloin.

creamy mushroom pasta

 preparation time 15 minutes • cooking time 15 minutes

12	ounces shell pasta
1/4	cup vegetable stock
1	clove garlic, crushed
1	pound button mushrooms, sliced thickly
1	cup frozen peas
4	scallions, sliced thinly
4	cups skim milk
2	rounded tablespoons cornstarch
3	tablespoons water
1/4	cup coarsely chopped fresh flat-leaf parsley
1 1/2	tablespoons whole-grain mustard
1/2	cup (2 ounces) freshly grated parmesan cheese
3	tablespoons finely chopped fresh chives

Skim milk keeps the fat count down but preserves the creamy taste. You can use any kind of short pasta you like – penne, rigatoni – in place of the shells.

1 Cook pasta in large pot of boiling water, uncovered, until just tender; drain, keep warm.

2 Bring stock to a boil in same cleaned pot; cook garlic and mushrooms, stirring, until mushrooms soften and liquid evaporates. Stir in peas and half of the scallions; cook, stirring, until scallions soften.

3 Add milk and blended cornstarch and water; cook, stirring, over low heat until sauce boils and thickens slightly.

4 Remove sauce from heat; stir in pasta, remaining scallions, parsley, mustard and cheese. Serve sprinkled with chives.

SERVES 4

per serving   3.8g fat; 359 calories
serving suggestion   Serve with crusty sourdough bread.

 tips Toss pasta through sauce just before serving – it will soak up all the sauce if tossed too early. Cremini, portobello or oyster mushrooms could be used instead of button.

pork rice-paper rolls

 preparation time 30 minutes • cooking time 5 minutes

12	ounces ground pork
1	clove garlic, crushed
1	teaspoon grated fresh ginger
1	teaspoon five-spice powder
12	ounces finely shredded Chinese cabbage
4	scallions, sliced thinly
1 1/2	tablespoons soy sauce
1/4	cup oyster sauce
1/4	cup tightly packed, coarsely chopped fresh cilantro leaves
12	9-inch rice paper sheets
1/4	cup sweet Thai chili sauce
3	tablespoons lime juice

When soaked in hot water, Vietnamese rice-paper sheets (*banh trang*) make pliable wrappers for a host of fillings. They can be found at Asian markets or in the international foods section of some supermarkets. You will need a small Chinese cabbage for this recipe.

SERVES 4
per serving
7.1g fat; 249 calories

tip Rolls can be prepared a day ahead. Cover; refrigerate.

1 Cook pork, garlic, ginger and spice in large non-stick skillet, stirring, until pork is changed in color and cooked through.

2 Add cabbage, onions, soy sauce, oyster sauce and 3 tablespoons of the cilantro to pan; cook, stirring, until cabbage is just wilted.

3 Place one sheet of rice paper in medium bowl of warm water until softened slightly; lift sheet carefully from water, place on cutting board, pat dry with paper towels. Place a twelfth of the filling mixture in center of sheet; fold in sides, roll top to bottom to enclose filling. Repeat with remaining rice paper sheets and filling.

4 Place rolls in single layer in large steamer set over large pot of simmering water; steam, covered, about 5 minutes or until just heated through. Serve rolls with dipping sauce made with combined remaining cilantro, chili sauce and juice.

fried rice

 preparation time 10 minutes • cooking time 10 minutes

2	eggs, beaten lightly
1	cooking-oil spray
4	ounces baby corn, halved
1	trimmed celery stalk, chopped finely
1	small red bell pepper, chopped finely
2	cloves garlic, crushed
5	ounces lean ham, chopped coarsely
3	cups cooked long-grain white rice
1 1/2	tablespoons ketjap manis
4	scallions, sliced thinly

Ketjap manis is a thick, sweet soy sauce that originated in Indonesia. It can be found in Asian markets, or you can make your own substitute by simmering equal parts soy sauce and molasses or brown sugar until the sugar is dissolved.
You need to cook 1 cup long-grain white rice several hours or a day before making this recipe; spread the still-warm cooked rice on a tray to cool, then cover and refrigerate until needed.

1 Pour eggs into heated medium non-stick skillet; cook, tilting pan, over medium heat until just set. Roll omelet then slice thinly; reserve.

2 Spray heated wok or large skillet lightly with cooking-oil spray; stir-fry corn and celery 2 minutes. Add bell pepper, garlic and ham; stir-fry 2 minutes. Add rice and ketjap manis; stir-fry until heated through. Stir in scallions and omelet; serve immediately.

SERVES 4

per serving
4.8g fat; 276 calories

serving suggestion
Serve with steamed greens
or stir-fried vegetables.

tip | A little chopped fresh chile can be added for a hint of spice.

penne with tomato salsa and tuna

 preparation time 15 minutes • cooking time 20 minutes

12	ounces penne
3	medium tomatoes (about 1 1/4 pounds), seeded, chopped finely
1	medium red onion, chopped finely
2	cloves garlic, crushed
1/4	cup firmly packed, torn fresh basil leaves
15	ounces canned tuna, drained, flaked
1/4	cup balsamic vinegar

The Italian name of this pasta means *pens*, a reference to the nib-like, pointy ends of each piece of pasta. Penne comes in both smooth (lisce) or ridged (rigate) versions, and a variety of sizes.

1 Cook pasta in large pot of boiling water, uncovered, until just tender; drain, keep warm.

2 Combine remaining ingredients in large bowl; add pasta, toss to combine.

SERVES 4

per serving
3.8g fat;
462 calories

serving suggestion
Serve with crusty
Italian bread and
a green salad.

tip You can substitute any pasta for the penne in this recipe.

rice with mushrooms and spinach

 preparation time 10 minutes • cooking time 25 minutes

3	cups vegetable stock
1/4	cup dry white wine
1 1/2	tablespoons finely grated lemon peel
1	medium onion, chopped finely
2	cloves garlic, crushed
8	ounces cremini mushrooms, halved
5	ounces button mushrooms, halved
1 1/2	cups medium-grain white rice
3	tablespoons lemon juice
1	cup water
3	cups baby spinach leaves, torn
1/2	cup (2 ounces) freshly grated parmesan cheese
3	tablespoons shredded fresh basil leaves

A simple covered cooking method replaces the usual labor-intensive non-stop stirring required in more traditional risottos. Best results will be achieved by using arborio rice, but you can use any medium-grain rice, as well.

SERVES 4
per serving
4.9g fat; 383 calories

serving suggestion
Olive or sourdough bread and a balsamic-dressed green salad turn this dish into a meal.

 Flat-leaf parsley can be substituted for the basil.

1 Heat 1 1/2 tablespoons of the stock with wine and peel in large pot, add onion and garlic; cook, stirring, until onion softens. Add mushrooms; cook, stirring, 5 minutes.

2 Stir in rice, juice, the water and remaining stock. Bring to a boil, reduce heat; simmer, covered, about 20 minutes or until rice is tender.

3 Just before serving, stir in spinach, cheese and basil.

rosemary lamb open sandwich

 preparation time 5 minutes (plus refrigeration time) • cooking time 15 minutes

2	cloves garlic, crushed
1/4	cup lemon juice
3	tablespoons fresh rosemary leaves
1 1/2	tablespoons whole-grain mustard
4	lamb tenderloins
2	small tomatoes
8	ounces asparagus, halved
4	slices light rye bread
3	cups Boston lettuce, chopped coarsely

SERVES 4

per serving   4.5g fat; 203 calories

serving suggestion
Dollop a spoonful of guacamole or low-fat mayonnaise, spiked with crushed garlic, on each sandwich.

tip You can substitute toasted sourdough or Italian for the rye bread.

1 Combine garlic, juice, rosemary and mustard in small bowl; toss lamb in marinade. Cover; refrigerate 3 hours or overnight.

2 Cut each tomato into six wedges. Cook tomatoes and asparagus, in batches, on heated oiled grill or grill pan until browned lightly and just tender. Toast bread on both sides.

3 Drain lamb; discard marinade. Cook lamb on same heated grill or grill pan until browned and cooked as desired. Cover; let stand 5 minutes before slicing thickly.

4 Place one slice of the toast on each serving plate; top each slice with equal amounts of lettuce, tomato, asparagus and lamb.

pasta and herb salad with lamb fillets

 preparation time 20 minutes • cooking time 10 minutes (plus standing time)

12	ounces bow-tie pasta (farfalle)
8	ounces yellow grape tomatoes, halved
1	medium red onion, sliced thinly
1 1/2	cups arugula leaves
1/4	cup loosely packed, finely shredded fresh basil leaves
1 1/2	tablespoons fresh thyme leaves
14	ounces lamb tenderloin
2	cloves garlic, crushed
1 1/2	tablespoons whole-grain mustard
1/4	cup balsamic vinegar

This salad can be served warm or cold. You can substitute your favorite pasta for the bow ties.

1 Cook pasta in large pot of boiling water, uncovered, until just tender; drain.

2 Combine tomatoes, onion, arugula, basil and thyme in large bowl.

3 Rub lamb all over with combined garlic and mustard; cook on heated oiled grill or grill pan until browned on both sides and cooked as desired. Let stand 5 minutes; slice thinly.

4 Add pasta, lamb and vinegar to vegetables; toss to combine.

SERVES 4

per serving 4.9g fat; 457 calories

serving suggestion
A crusty bread is a good partner for this salad.

gazpacho

 preparation time 10 minutes (plus standing time) • cooking time 10 minutes

2	medium red bell peppers
4	cups vegetable juice
3	tablespoons red wine vinegar
1/2	teaspoon Tabasco sauce
1	clove garlic, quartered
3	trimmed stalks celery, chopped finely
1	medium red onion, chopped finely
5	medium tomatoes (about 2 pounds), chopped finely
2	hothouse cucumbers (about 1 3/4 pounds), peeled, seeded, chopped finely

The cooks of Andalusia devised this refreshing chilled soup, possibly as an antidote to the passions aroused by those other contributions to Spanish culture – flamenco and bullfighting. Often called a pureed salad, gazpacho sometimes has stale breadcrumbs blended in with the vegetables to make it a heartier meal.

SERVES 8

per serving
0.4g fat; 64 calories

serving suggestion
serve in glass tumblers
with a celery swizzle stick.

tip Traditional accompaniments for this soup include croutons and diced hard-boiled egg.

1 Quarter bell peppers; remove and discard seeds and membranes. Roast under broiler, skin-side up, until skin blisters and blackens. Cover pepper pieces with plastic wrap or aluminum foil 5 minutes. Peel away and discard skin; chop peppers coarsely.

2 Blend or process bell peppers with vegetable juice, vinegar, Tabasco, garlic and half of the celery, onion, tomatoes and cucumbers until smooth; transfer mixture to large bowl. Cover; refrigerate about 1 hour or until cold. Refrigerate remaining half of the chopped vegetables.

3 Divide gazpacho among serving dishes; top each with reserved chopped vegetables just before serving.

chicken, noodle and oyster-mushroom stir-fry

 preparation time 15 minutes • cooking time 15 minutes

1	pound Asian stir-fry noodles
1	pound boneless, skinless chicken thighs, chopped coarsely
1	clove garlic, crushed
7	ounces broccoli florets
5	ounces oyster mushrooms, halved
1	medium red onion, sliced thinly
7	ounces snow peas, halved
1/4	cup oyster sauce

You will need about 1 3/4 pounds of broccoli to yield the florets for this recipe.
Asian stir-fry (Hokkien) noodles are sold in Asian markets and some supermarkets.

1 Rinse noodles under hot water; drain. Transfer to large bowl; separate noodles with fork.

2 Stir-fry chicken in heated lightly oiled wok or large skillet, in batches, until browned all over and cooked through.

3 Stir-fry garlic, broccoli, mushrooms and onion in same pan until onion just softens. Return chicken to wok with noodles, snow peas and sauce; stir-fry until vegetables are just tender.

SERVES 4

per serving
10.9g fat; 565 calories

serving suggestion
Serve with a side dish of chopped fresh chiles or Asian hot sauce to add heat to the noodles.

sweet chili chicken with rice

 preparation time 10 minutes (plus refrigeration time) • cooking time 15 minutes

2	teaspoons grated fresh ginger
3	cloves garlic, crushed
1	stalk fresh lemongrass, chopped finely
1/4	cup sweet Thai chili sauce
1/4	cup lime juice
1/2	cup loosely packed, coarsely chopped fresh cilantro leaves
4	boneless, skinless chicken breasts (about 1 1/2 pounds)
3/4	cup long-grain white rice
1	cup chicken stock
2	teaspoons cornstarch

Garlic, lemongrass and sweet Thai chili sauce lend a Thai accent to this recipe.

1 Combine ginger, garlic, lemongrass, sauce, juice and half of the cilantro in large bowl; toss chicken in marinade. Cover; refrigerate 3 hours or overnight.

2 Drain chicken over large bowl; reserve marinade. Cook chicken, uncovered, in heated large non-stick skillet until browned on both sides and cooked through; slice chicken thickly.

3 Boil, steam or microwave rice until just tender; drain, if necessary, then stir in remaining cilantro.

4 Meanwhile, blend 3 tablespoons of the stock with cornstarch in measuring cup. Place remaining stock in medium pot with reserved marinade; bring to a boil. Reduce heat; simmer, stir in cornstarch mixture. Cook, stirring, about 5 minutes or until sauce boils and thickens.

5 Serve chicken on rice; drizzle with sauce.

SERVES 4

per serving   10.3g fat; 398 calories

serving suggestion   Serve with stir-fried Asian greens such as kale or bok choy.

tip Lemongrass can be found in Asian markets; buy it fresh, not frozen or dried. Use only the lower white part of each stem of lemongrass. Alternatively, you can substitute grated lemon peel; the peel of one lemon is equivalent to two stalks of lemongrass.

preparation time 15 minutes (plus refrigeration time) • cooking time 15 minutes

8	chicken tenderloins (1 1/4 pounds)
1/3	cup honey
3	tablespoons whole-grain mustard
1/3	cup white vinegar
3	tablespoons soy sauce
3	medium potatoes (about 1 1/4 pounds)
1	small sweet potato
2	cloves garlic, sliced thinly
1/4	cup skim milk
2	teaspoons fresh thyme leaves

Soak eight bamboo skewers in water for at least an hour before use to prevent them from splintering or scorching. The honey-mustard marinade is also used to make the sauce in this recipe.

SERVES 4
per serving
8.7g fat; 441 calories

serving suggestion
Serve with steamed green vegetables or a green salad.

tips You can grill or barbecue the chicken rather than bake it.
Spray the tablespoon with cooking-oil spray to make the honey easier to measure.

1 Thread each piece of chicken onto a bamboo skewer; place in shallow baking dish. Combine honey, mustard, vinegar and sauce; pour over chicken. Cover; refrigerate 3 hours or overnight.

2 Preheat oven to 425.

3 Roast undrained chicken, uncovered, about 10 minutes or until cooked through.

4 Meanwhile, boil, steam or microwave combined potatoes, sweet potato and garlic until tender; drain. Mash in medium bowl with milk; stir in thyme. Heat remaining marinade in small pot.

5 Serve chicken with mashed potatoes; drizzle with marinade.

breaded fish with warm tomato salad

 preparation time 15 minutes • cooking time 25 minutes

1	cooking-oil spray
1	medium red onion
8	ounces cherry tomatoes
1/4	cup white wine vinegar
2	cloves garlic, crushed
1/3	cup crushed corn flakes
1	teaspoon ground cumin
1	teaspoon sweet paprika
1	teaspoon ground turmeric
4	firm white fish fillets (1 1/2 pounds)
1/4	cup flour
2	egg whites, beaten lightly
5	cups baby spinach leaves
1/4	cup drained capers

You can use snapper, cod, bream or any other firm white fish in this recipe.

SERVES 4

per serving
5.6g fat; 317 calories

 tip Fish can be breaded 2 hours before cooking time. Cover; refrigerate.

1 Preheat oven to 425. Spray baking pan lightly with cooking-oil spray.

2 Cut onion into thin wedges. Place onion and tomatoes on prepared pan; drizzle with combined vinegar and garlic. Roast, uncovered, about 20 minutes or until tomatoes are softened.

3 Combine crumbs and spices in small bowl.

4 Meanwhile, coat fish in flour; shake away excess. Dip fish in egg white, then coat in crumb mixture. Spray fish on both sides with cooking-oil spray; cook, uncovered, in heated large non-stick skillet until browned on both sides and cooked through.

5 Combine spinach and capers in large bowl with tomato and onion mixture; serve with fish.

tuna and asparagus frittata

 preparation time 10 minutes • cooking time 30 minutes

5	medium potatoes (about 2 pounds), sliced thinly
1	medium onion, sliced thinly
1	clove garlic, crushed
8	ounces asparagus, trimmed, chopped coarsely
15	ounces canned tuna, drained
4	eggs, beaten lightly
4	egg whites, beaten lightly
3	tablespoons finely chopped fresh flat-leaf parsley
1	cooking-oil spray

1 Boil, steam or microwave potato until almost tender.

2 Cook onion and garlic in heated small, ovenproof non-stick skillet, stirring, until onion softens.

3 Combine potatoes and onion mixture in large bowl with asparagus, tuna, eggs, egg whites and parsley.

4 Reheat same pan; spray lightly with cooking-oil spray. Spoon frittata mixture into pan, press down firmly; cook, uncovered, over low heat until almost set. Remove from heat; place under heated broiler until frittata sets and top is browned lightly.

A frittata, Italian in origin, is a type of omelet cooked in a skillet, either on top of the stove or in the oven until set through. It makes great picnic fare or a welcome addition to the antipasto plate.

SERVES 4

per serving
8.2g fat; 358 calories

serving suggestion
Serve with a mixed-greens salad drizzled with balsamic vinegar.

tip Substitute well-drained canned asparagus for the fresh, if desired.

salmon and roast potato salad

 preparation time 10 minutes • cooking time 30 minutes (plus cooling time)

1	pound fingerling potatoes, chopped coarsely
15	-ounce can pink salmon
2	medium tomatoes, cut into wedges
1	small head romaine lettuce, torn roughly
1/2	cup sour cream
1	medium red onion, chopped finely
1/4	cup drained capers, chopped finely
3	tablespoons finely chopped fresh dill
3	tablespoons lemon juice

1 Preheat oven to 425. Lightly oil large baking dish.

2 Place potato in prepared dish; roast, uncovered, stirring occasionally, about 30 minutes or until browned and crisp. Allow potato to cool.

3 Drain salmon; remove any bones and skin, then flake with fork in large serving bowl.

4 Place cooled potato in bowl with salmon; add tomatoes and lettuce, toss to combine. Drizzle with combined remaining ingredients just before serving.

SERVES 4

per serving   17.6g fat; 344 calories

smoked chicken salad

 preparation time 15 minutes

14	ounces smoked chicken breast
7	cups baby spinach
1	medium yellow bell pepper, sliced thinly
1	medium red onion, sliced thinly
1	cup firmly packed fresh basil
2	teaspoons finely grated lime peel
1/4	cup lime juice
3	tablespoons coarsely chopped fresh cilantro
2	red Serrano or Thai chilies, seeded, chopped finely
2	teaspoons peanut oil
1	teaspoon sugar

Smoked chicken has already been cooked during the curing process, making this a simple salad to put together on short notice. You can keep smoked chicken in your freezer; just thaw before slicing.

SERVES 8

per serving
3.9g fat; 87 calories

serving suggestion
serve with cornbread
or flour tortillas.

1 Remove and discard any skin from chicken; slice chicken thinly.

2 Combine chicken, spinach, bell pepper, onion and basil in large bowl.

3 Whisk together remaining ingredients.

4 Pour dressing over salad; toss gently to combine.

tuna bean salad

 preparation time 15 minutes

2	cups mixed salad greens
15	ounces canned tuna, drained, flaked
14	-ounce can butter beans, rinsed, drained
1	small red onion, sliced finely
8	ounces yellow grape tomatoes
1/2	cup low-fat Italian dressing
3	tablespoons coarsely chopped fresh flat-leaf parsley
3	tablespoons coarsely chopped fresh basil leaves

1 Divide salad greens among four serving bowls.

2 Combine remaining ingredients in large bowl; divide among lettuce-lined serving bowls.

SERVES 4

per serving
11.7g fat; 244 calories

tip This recipe is best made close to serving time.

cajun beef roll

 preparation time 10 minutes • cooking time 25 minutes

1	pound top round or sirloin steak, sliced thinly
1	medium onion, sliced thinly
1	medium red bell pepper, sliced thinly
3	tablespoons Cajun seasoning
3	medium tomatoes (about 1 1/4 pounds)
1	long loaf French bread

1 Heat oiled large skillet; cook beef, in batches, until beef is browned and cooked as desired. Remove from pan.

2 Add onion to same skillet with bell pepper and seasoning; cook, stirring, until onion is browned lightly. Cut each tomato into eight wedges, add to pan; simmer, uncovered, 15 minutes or until mixture thickens.

3 Return beef to pan; toss gently to combine with tomato mixture.

4 Trim ends from bread; quarter the loaf, then split pieces almost all the way through. Line bread with lettuce leaves, if desired. Divide beef mixture among bread rolls just before serving.

SERVES 4

per serving
9.5g fat; 421 calories

tip This recipe is best made close to serving time.

sesame chicken salad

 preparation time 15 minutes (plus cooling time)
• cooking time 15 minutes

4	split (bone-in) chicken breasts (2 pounds), skin removed
6	cups chicken stock
2	star anise
1 1/2	tablespoons light soy sauce
1	teaspoon sesame oil
7	ounces snow peas, halved
3 1/2	ounces mung bean sprouts
2	cups bean sprouts
2	trimmed celery stalks, sliced finely
4	scallions, sliced finely
1 1/2	tablespoons sesame seeds, toasted

DRESSING

3	tablespoons soy sauce
1 1/2	tablespoons peanut oil
2	teaspoons sesame oil
1/2	teaspoon grated fresh ginger

1 Place chicken in large pot with stock, star anise, soy sauce and oil. Bring to a boil; simmer, uncovered, 10 minutes. Cool chicken in stock. Drain over large bowl; reserve stock for another use. Remove chicken meat from bone, slice thickly.

2 Meanwhile, plunge peas into pot of boiling water; drain immediately. Plunge into bowl of ice water and let stand 2 minutes; drain.

3 Whisk together ingredients for dressing.

4 Combine chicken, peas, sprouts, celery, scallions and dressing in large bowl; top with sesame seeds.

SERVES 4

per serving
20g fat; 405 calories

 tip Chicken can be cooked a day ahead; cover, refrigerate.

NIBBLES

Satisfy the munchies and keep a clear conscience about your health with this crunchy collection.

fruit nibble mix

preparation time 10 minutes • cooking time 5 minutes

3	rice cakes, crumbled
1/2	cup puffed wheat
1/2	teaspoon sesame oil
2	teaspoons teriyaki sauce
1 1/2	tablespoons honey
12	small breadsticks
1/4	cup dried apricots, halved
1/4	cup dried apples, halved
1/4	cup dried dates, pitted, chopped coarsely
1/4	cup golden raisins

1. Preheat oven to 425.

2. Combine rice cakes, puffed wheat, oil, teriyaki sauce and honey in medium bowl; spread mixture in even layer on baking pan. Roast, uncovered, about 5 minutes or until just crisp and toasted, stirring occasionally.

3. Break breadsticks into small pieces; place in large bowl with cooled rice cake mixture and remaining ingredients. Toss gently to combine.

SERVES 4

per serving 1.8g fat; 185 calories

mustard munch

preparation time 10 minutes • cooking time 20 minutes

4	rice cakes
2	ounces sesame rice crackers
1	cup puffed wheat
1	cup puffed rice
1	egg white, beaten lightly
2	teaspoons salt
1	teaspoon ground turmeric
2	teaspoons sweet paprika
2	teaspoons mustard powder
1 1/2	tablespoons whole-grain mustard

1. Preheat oven to 325. Lightly oil baking pan. Break rice cakes and crackers into pieces.

2. Combine rice cakes, crackers, puffed wheat and puffed rice in bowl; stir in egg white, salt, spices and mustard.

3. Spread mixture onto prepared pan; roast, uncovered, about 20 minutes or until mustard munch is crisp.

SERVES 4

per serving 2.4g fat; 151 calories

spiced popcorn

preparation time 5 minutes • cooking time 20 minutes

1/2	cup popcorn
2	teaspoons ground cumin
2	teaspoons ground coriander
1	teaspoon ground cinnamon

1. Pop popcorn in an air popper.

2. Cook combined spices in small, dry heated skillet until fragrant.

3. Place popcorn in large bowl with spice mixture; toss gently to combine.

MAKES 12 CUPS

per 1/2-cup serving 0.4g fat; 32 calories

tips If you don't have an air popper, place popcorn in an oven bag or paper bag; secure bag loosely with kitchen string. Microwave at MEDIUM-HIGH (70%) for about 4 minutes or until popped. Remove bag from microwave oven with tongs; let stand for 2 minutes before opening bag.

MAINS

These grills, bakes, pastas, curries and stir-fries come complete with accompaniments, for easy menu planning and preparation, and for keeping track of fat and calorie counts.

satay beef stir-fry with Asian noodles

 preparation time 15 minutes • cooking time 15 minutes

1 1/4	pounds Asian (hokkien) noodles
10	ounces boneless beef sirloin, sliced thinly
1/2	teaspoon finely grated fresh ginger
2	teaspoons sesame oil
1	small red onion, sliced thinly
1	medium red bell pepper, sliced thinly
5	ounces broccoli florets
2	teaspoons lime juice
1/4	cup satay sauce
1 1/2	tablespoons hoisin sauce
1/3	cup soy sauce
1 1/2	tablespoons ketjap manis
5	ounces snow peas
1 1/2	tablespoons finely chopped fresh cilantro leaves
1/4	cup unsalted roasted peanuts, chopped coarsely

Ketjap manis, a thick sweet soy sauce of Indonesian origin, is available at some supermarkets and Asian food stores. You can also make your own substitute by combining equal parts soy sauce and molasses or brown sugar, then boiling the mixture until the sugar dissolves.

SERVES 4

per serving
15.8g fat; 670 calories

serving suggestion
Serve with a bowl of
hot Asian chili sauce.

1 Rinse noodles under hot water; drain. Transfer to large bowl; separate noodles with fork.

2 Heat oiled wok or large non-stick skillet; stir-fry beef and ginger, in batches, until browned.

3 Heat oil in same wok; stir-fry onion, bell pepper and broccoli until just tender. Return beef to wok with combined juice and sauces; stir-fry until sauce boils. Add noodles and snow peas; stir-fry until hot.

4 Add cilantro; stir-fry until combined. Serve sprinkled with peanuts.

veal with swirled mashed potatoes

 preparation time 10 minutes • cooking time 20 minutes

1	pound veal steaks
1/3	cup flour
1	egg white, beaten lightly
3	tablespoons skim milk
1	cup crushed corn flakes
1	teaspoon finely grated lemon peel
3	tablespoons finely chopped fresh flat-leaf parsley
1	cooking-oil spray
4	medium potatoes (about 1 3/4 pounds)
1/4	cup buttermilk
3/4	cup chicken stock
2	cups frozen peas
1	lemon, cut into 8 wedges

There's not a hint of deprivation in this satisfying combination of veal and mashed potatoes.

1 Preheat oven to 475. Lightly oil baking pan.

2 Cut each steak in half. Toss veal in flour; shake away excess. Dip veal in combined egg white and milk, then coat in combined crumbs, lemon peel and parsley.

3 Place veal in single layer on prepared pan; spray lightly with cooking-oil spray. Bake, uncovered, about 5 minutes or until cooked through. Let stand 5 minutes; slice thickly.

4 Meanwhile, boil, steam or microwave potatoes until soft; drain. Mash potatoes with buttermilk in medium bowl; cover to keep warm.

5 Place stock in medium pot; bring to a boil. Add peas; cook, uncovered, until stock reduces by half. Blend or process until pea mixture is almost pureed.

6 Gently swirl pea mixture into mash potatoes to give marbled effect. Divide potatoes among plates; top with veal. Serve with lemon.

SERVES 4

per serving 4.3g fat; 515 calories

serving suggestion   Serve with a contrasting-colored vegetable such as boiled or steamed carrots, corn on the cob, or oven-roasted tomatoes.

 tip Veal can be breaded several hours ahead; store, covered, in refrigerator.

pork with ratatouille and potatoes

 preparation time 10 minutes • cooking time 25 minutes

2	pounds tiny new potatoes, halved
1	medium onion, chopped coarsely
2	cloves garlic, crushed
4	baby eggplants, chopped coarsely
2	medium green zucchini, chopped coarsely
14	-ounce can crushed tomatoes, undrained
3	tablespoons finely shredded fresh basil leaves
4	5-ounce pork steaks

1 Preheat oven to 475.

2 Place potatoes in large lightly oiled baking dish; roast, uncovered, about 25 minutes or until browned and crisp.

3 Meanwhile, cook onion and garlic in heated large non-stick skillet, stirring, until onion softens. Stir in eggplant and zucchini; cook, stirring, until vegetables are just tender.

4 Stir in tomatoes; bring to a boil. Reduce heat; simmer, uncovered, about 5 minutes or until vegetables are tender and sauce thickens. Stir in basil.

5 Cook pork, in batches, in heated medium non-stick skillet until browned on both sides and cooked as desired. Slice pork thickly.

6 Serve pork with potatoes and ratatouille.

SERVES 4

per serving 6.2g fat; 395 calories

serving suggestion A green salad goes well with this dish.

tip Ratatouille can be made a day ahead; store, covered, in refrigerator. It is great on its own, or served with pasta.

In a Provençale dialect, *touiller* means to stir and crush, thus the name ratatouille perfectly describes this rich vegetable stew.

pork fillet with apples and leeks

 preparation time 10 minutes • cooking time 25 minutes

1 3/4	pounds pork steaks
3/4	cup chicken stock
2	medium leeks (about 1 1/2 pounds), sliced thickly
1	clove garlic, crushed
3	tablespoons brown sugar
3	tablespoons red wine vinegar
2	medium apples
1	tablespoon butter
1 1/2	tablespoons brown sugar
1	pound baby carrots, halved
8	baby yellow or scalloped squash (only 3 ounces total), quartered
8	ounces asparagus, trimmed, coarsely chopped

Pork has a natural affinity with both apples and onions; here, these traditional accompaniments are given a contemporary twist

SERVES 4

per serving
7.5g fat; 393 calories

serving suggestion
Potatoes – boiled, mashed or baked – would make a good accompaniment for this dish.

tip You can make the sweet-and-sour leek several hours ahead; just reheat before serving.

1 Preheat oven to 475.

2 Place pork, in single layer, in large baking dish; bake, uncovered, about 25 minutes or until pork is browned and cooked as desired. Cover; let stand 5 minutes before slicing thickly.

3 Meanwhile, heat half of the stock in medium skillet; cook leek and garlic, stirring, until leek softens and browns slightly. Add 3 table-spoons sugar and vinegar; cook, stirring, about 5 minutes or until leek caramelizes. Add remaining stock; bring to a boil. Reduce heat; simmer, uncovered, about 5 minutes or until liquid reduces by half. Place leek mixture in medium bowl; cover to keep warm.

4 Peel, core and halve apples; cut into thick slices.

5 Melt butter in same pan; cook apples and 1 1/2 tablespoons sugar, stirring, until apples are browned and tender.

6 Boil, steam or microwave carrots, squash and asparagus, separately, until just tender; drain.

7 Serve pork, topped with caramelized apples and sweet-and-sour leek, on top of the mixed vegetables.

garbanzo and squash curry

 preparation time 10 minutes • cooking time 25 minutes

2	teaspoons peanut oil
2	medium onions, sliced thinly
2	cloves garlic, crushed
3	tablespoons tikka masala curry paste
2	cups vegetable stock
1	cup water
2	pounds butternut squash, chopped coarsely
2	cups jasmine rice
10	-ounce can garbanzos, rinsed, drained
1	cup frozen peas
1/4	cup half and half
3	tablespoons chopped fresh cilantro leaves

1 Heat oil in large pot; cook onion and garlic, stirring, until onion softens. Add paste; cook, stirring, until fragrant. Stir in stock and the water; bring to a boil. Add squash; reduce heat. Simmer, covered, 15 minutes or until squash is almost tender.

2 Meanwhile, cook rice in large pot of boiling water, uncovered, until tender; drain. Cover to keep warm.

3 Add garbanzos and peas to curry; cook, stirring, until hot. Stir in cream and cilantro. Serve curry with rice.

In Indian cooking, the word *masala* loosely translates as *paste*; the word *tikka* refers to a bite-sized piece of meat, poultry, fish or vegetable. Tikka masala sauce contains spices and oils, mixed to a mild paste. You can find it on the international foods aisle of your supermarket.

SERVES 4

per serving 12.5g fat; 629 calories

serving suggestion Serve with a fresh chutney, Indian bread and yogurt, if desired.

tip Make the curry a day ahead to allow the flavors to develop.

steak bourguignon with celeriac-mashed potatoes

preparation time 10 minutes • cooking time 20 minutes

1	small celeriac (about 1 1/4 pounds), chopped coarsely
2	medium potatoes, chopped coarsely
1/4	cup skim milk
1 1/2	tablespoons butter
4	7-ounce beef tenderloin steaks
7	ounces button mushrooms, halved
6	baby onions, quartered
2	cloves garlic, crushed
1/2	cup dry red wine
1	cup beef stock
1 1/2	tablespoons tomato paste
2	teaspoons cornstarch
2	teaspoons water
1 1/2	tablespoons coarsely chopped fresh oregano

You can substitute fillet mignon or New York sirloin steak for the tenderloin in this recipe.

1 Boil, steam or microwave celeriac and potato, separately, until tender; drain. Mash in medium bowl with milk and butter, cover to keep warm.

2 Meanwhile, cook beef in heated large non-stick skillet until browned on both sides and cooked as desired; cover to keep warm.

3 Cook mushrooms, onions and garlic in same pan until vegetables just soften. Add wine, stock and paste; simmer, uncovered, about 5 minutes. Stir in blended cornstarch and water; cook, stirring, until sauce boils and thickens.

4 Serve beef with mashed potatoes and bourguignon sauce; sprinkle with oregano.

SERVES 4

per serving 14.3g fat; 444 calories
serving suggestion Serve with steamed green vegetables such as asparagus or broccoli.

tip Mashed potatoes and celeriac can be made a day ahead and kept, covered, in refrigerator; reheat just before serving. Incidentally, mashed potatoes respond well to being reheated in a microwave oven.

fettuccine bolognese

 preparation time 5 minutes • cooking time 25 minutes

1   small onion,
    chopped finely
2   cloves garlic, crushed
1   small carrot,
    chopped finely
1   trimmed celery stalk,
    chopped finely
14 ounces lean ground
    beef
2   cups bottled tomato
    pasta sauce
1/2 cup beef stock
12 ounces fettuccine

SERVES 4

per serving
10.2g fat; 565 calories

serving suggestion
Serve with a green salad and
a loaf of crusty Italian bread.

 tip   The flavor of the bolognese will improve if it is
made a day ahead; reheat
just before serving.

1 Cook onion and garlic in heated large non-stick skillet, stirring, until onion softens. Add carrot and celery; cook, stirring, until vegetables are just tender.

2 Add beef; cook, stirring, until no longer pink. Add sauce and stock; bring to a boil. Reduce heat; simmer, uncovered, about 15 minutes or until mixture thickens slightly.

3 Meanwhile, cook pasta in large pot of boiling water, uncovered, until just tender; drain.

4 Serve fettuccine topped with bolognese sauce.

gnocchi with herb and mushroom sauce

 preparation time 10 minutes · cooking time 15 minutes

1 1/2	tablespoons vegetable oil
1	medium onion, chopped coarsely
2	cloves garlic, crushed
14	ounces cremini mushrooms, sliced thinly
1 1/2	tablespoons flour
1/3	cup dry red wine
2	teaspoons soy sauce
2/3	cup vegetable stock
1 1/2	tablespoons light sour cream
1 1/2	tablespoons coarsely chopped fresh oregano
1 1/2	tablespoons finely chopped fresh sage
1 1/4	pounds fresh potato gnocchi

Gnocchi are small dumplings made of ingredients such as flour, potatoes, semolina, ricotta cheese or spinach. They make a great base for a full-flavored sauce such as this - packed with herbs, red wine and mushrooms.

SERVES 4
per serving
7.6g fat; 334 calories

serving suggestion
Serve with a green salad, dressed with herb vinaigrette, and fresh crusty bread.

tip You could substitute button or oyster mushrooms for the cremini.

1 Heat oil in large skillet; cook onion, garlic and mushrooms, stirring, until vegetables are just tender. Add flour; cook, stirring, 1 minute.

2 Add wine, sauce, stock and cream; cook, stirring, until sauce thickens slightly. Stir in herbs.

3 Meanwhile, cook gnocchi in large pot of boiling water, uncovered, until gnocchi rise to the surface and are just tender; drain. Add gnocchi to herb and mushroom sauce; toss gently to combine.

mustard veal with polenta and spinach purée

 preparation time 15 minutes • cooking time 20 minutes

1/3	cup whole-grain mustard
3	tablespoons coarsely chopped fresh oregano
2	cloves garlic, crushed
4	veal chops (1 1/4 pounds)
4	large plum tomatoes, halved
2	cups water
1	teaspoon salt
1	cup polenta
3/4	cup skim milk
1/4	cup (1 ounce) freshly grated parmesan cheese
4 1/2	pounds spinach, trimmed
2	cloves garlic, crushed, extra
2	anchovy fillets, drained
3	tablespoons lemon juice
1/4	cup beef stock

Polenta is the Italian answer to mashed potatoes – the perfect accompaniment for soaking up meat juices and too-good-to-waste sauces.

SERVES 4

per serving
7.3g fat; 389 calories

serving suggestion
Top steaks with fresh sage leaves, and serve with a radicchio or arugula salad dressed in balsamic vinegar.

 tip — Fresh rosemary or thyme can be substituted for the oregano.

1 Combine mustard, oregano and garlic in small bowl; brush veal on both sides with mustard mixture.

2 Cook veal and tomato, in batches, on heated lightly oiled grill or grill pan until veal is browned on both sides and cooked as desired and tomato is browned and tender.

3 Meanwhile, bring combined water and salt to a boil in medium pot. Stir in polenta; cook, stirring, about 10 minutes or until polenta thickens. Stir in milk; cook, stirring, about 5 minutes or until polenta thickens. Stir in cheese.

4 Boil, steam or microwave spinach until just wilted; squeeze out excess liquid with hands. Blend or process spinach with remaining ingredients until pureed.

5 Serve veal chops with tomato, polenta and pureed spinach.

beef steak with bell-pepper relish

 preparation time 10 minutes • cooking time 20 minutes

3	medium red bell peppers (about 1 1/4 pounds)
1	teaspoon olive oil
1	large onion, sliced thinly
2	cloves garlic, sliced thinly
3	tablespoons brown sugar
3	tablespoons sherry vinegar
3	red serrano or Thai chiles, seeded, chopped finely
4	7-ounce beef tenderloin steaks
2	ears fresh corn, shucked, chopped coarsely
5	ounces sugar snap peas
10 1/2	ounces tiny new potatoes, halved
3	tablespoons finely chopped fresh flat-leaf parsley

You can substitute fillet mignon or New York sirloin steak for the tenderloin in this recipe.

1 Quarter bell peppers; remove and discard seeds and membranes. Roast under broiler, skin-side up, until skin blisters and blackens. Cover with plastic wrap or aluminum foil for 5 minutes; peel away skin, slice thinly.

2 Heat oil in medium skillet; cook onion and garlic, stirring, until soft. Add sugar, vinegar, chile and bell peppers; cook, stirring, 5 minutes.

3 Meanwhile, cook beef on heated oiled grill or grill pan until browned and cooked as desired.

4 Boil, steam or microwave vegetables, separately, until just tender; drain.

5 Top steaks with bell-pepper relish; serve with vegetables, sprinkle with parsley.

SERVES 4

per serving
13g fat; 557 calories

serving suggestion
Serve with a green salad with vinaigrette.

 You can make the bell-pepper relish a day ahead; store, covered, in refrigerator. Reheat just before serving.

cauliflower vegetable curry

preparation time 10 minutes • cooking time 20 minutes

1	medium onion, sliced thickly
2	red serrano or Thai chiles, chopped coarsely
1	clove garlic, crushed
3	tablespoons mild curry paste
4	small potatoes (about 1 pound), chopped coarsely
1	pound cauliflower florets
1 1/2	cups vegetable stock
1 1/2	cups water
2	cups jasmine rice
7	ounces green beans, halved
1 1/3	cups light coconut milk
4	hard-boiled eggs, sliced thickly
1/4	cup loosely packed fresh cilantro leaves

1 Cook onion, chile and garlic in heated large non-stick pot, stirring, until onion softens. Stir in paste; cook, stirring, until fragrant. Add potato and cauliflower; cook, stirring, until coated in curry mixture. Add stock and the water; bring to a boil. Reduce heat; simmer, covered, about 10 minutes or until potato is just tender.

2 Meanwhile, cook rice in large pot of boiling water, uncovered, until just tender; drain. Cover to keep warm.

3 Stir beans into curry mixture; cook, uncovered, until just tender. Stir in coconut milk and egg; simmer, uncovered, until hot. Serve curry with rice; sprinkle with cilantro.

Contrasting colors add eye appeal to this fragrant curry, which would traditionally be served with Indian flat breads such as naan or puri. You can substitute equivalent amounts of peas, bell peppers, mushrooms or zucchini if you prefer them to the vegetables suggested in the recipe.

SERVES 4

per serving
16.6g fat; 679 calories

serving suggestion
Serve with raita made with low-fat yogurt and cucumber, and Indian curry.

garlic shrimp and bok choy with herbed rice

 preparation time 20 minutes • cooking time 15 minutes

36	medium uncooked shrimp (2 pounds)
6	cloves garlic, crushed
2	teaspoons finely chopped fresh cilantro
3	red Serrano or Thai chilies, seeded, chopped finely
1/3	cup lime juice
1	teaspoon sugar
1 1/2	tablespoons peanut oil
2	pounds baby bok choy, quartered lengthwise
6	green onions, sliced thinly
1 1/2	tablespoons sweet Thai chili sauce

HERBED RICE

2	cups jasmine rice
3	tablespoons coarsely chopped fresh cilantro
1 1/2	tablespoons coarsely chopped fresh mint
1 1/2	tablespoons coarsely chopped fresh flat-leaf parsley
1	teaspoon finely grated lime peel

SERVES 6

per serving
4.5g fat; 383 calories

1 Peel and devein shrimp, leaving tails intact.

2 Combine shrimp in large bowl with garlic, cilantro, chili, lime juice and sugar.

3 Heat half of the oil in wok or large non-stick skillet; stir-fry shrimp, in batches, until just changed in color.

4 Heat remaining oil with pan juices in wok; stir-fry bok choy, onions and chili sauce, in batches, until just tender. Combine bok choy mixture and shrimp in wok; stir-fry until hot. Serve shrimp on herbed rice.

HERBED RICE Cook rice, uncovered, in large pot of boiling water until tender; drain. Return rice to pan; combine with remaining ingredients

vegetable and tofu stir-fry

 preparation time 10 minutes • cooking time 15 minutes

8	ounces fresh firm tofu
8	ounces fresh rice noodles
1 1/2	tablespoons peanut oil
1	large onion, sliced thickly
2	cloves garlic, crushed
1	teaspoon five-spice powder
10	ounces button mushrooms, halved
7	ounces cremini mushrooms, halved
1/4	cup soy sauce
1	cup vegetable stock
1/4	cup water
10	ounces baby bok choy, chopped coarsely
10	ounces choy sum, chopped coarsely
4	scallions, chopped coarsely
7	ounce bean sprouts

Tofu, also known as bean curd, is made from the "milk" of crushed soy beans. Its fairly mild flavor is enhanced by the vegetables and sauce.

 1 Cut tofu into 3/4-inch cubes. Rinse noodles under hot water; drain. Transfer to large bowl; separate noodles with fork.

2 Heat oil in wok or large skillet; stir-fry onion and garlic until onion softens. Add five-spice; stir-fry until fragrant. Add mushrooms; stir-fry until almost tender.

3 Add combined sauce, stock and the water; bring to a boil. Add bok choy, choy sum and scallions; stir-fry until bok choy just wilts. Add tofu, noodles and sprouts; stir-fry until hot.

SERVES 4

per serving 9.3g fat; 316 calories

tip You can use rice stick noodles if fresh noodles are not available. Place rice stick noodles in a large heatproof bowl; cover with boiling water. Let stand until just tender; drain.

spaghetti with tomato and white beans

 preparation time 10 minutes • cooking time 20 minutes

1/3	cup vegetable stock
1	small red onion, chopped finely
2	cloves garlic, crushed
1	cup dry white wine
1/2	teaspoon sugar
2	cups bottled tomato pasta sauce
12	ounces spaghetti
1 1/2	tablespoons coarsely chopped fresh oregano
3	tablespoons drained capers, chopped coarsely
1/2	cup seeded black olives, quartered
10 1/2	-ounce can butter beans, rinsed, drained
3	tablespoons coarsely chopped fresh flat-leaf parsley

Beans are an Italian staple and are often served with spaghetti, that other great favorite, in the same dish.

1 Heat half the stock in medium pot; cook onion and garlic, stirring, until onion softens. Stir in wine, remaining stock, sugar and sauce; bring to a boil. Reduce heat; simmer, uncovered, until sauce thickens slightly.

2 Cook pasta in large pot of boiling water, uncovered, until just tender; drain.

3 Meanwhile, stir remaining ingredients into sauce; cook, stirring, until hot. Serve spaghetti with tomato and white bean sauce.

SERVES 4

per serving 2.4g fat; 464 calories

serving suggestion
If you are not overly concerned about fat counts, serve with parmesan.

 tip Make sauce a day ahead; store, covered, in refrigerator.

phad thai

 preparation time 15 minutes • cooking time 15 minutes

8	ounces rice stick noodles
1	pound boneless, skinless chicken thighs, sliced thinly
1	clove garlic, crushed
1	teaspoon grated fresh ginger
2	red serrano or Thai chiles, sliced thinly
2	tablespoons brown sugar
3	tablespoons soy sauce
1/4	cup sweet Thai chili sauce
1 1/2	tablespoons fish sauce
1 1/2	tablespoons lime juice
3	scallions, sliced thinly
1	cup bean sprouts
1	cup snow pea sprouts
1/4	cup loosely packed, coarsely chopped fresh cilantro leaves

Noodles are a favorite Thai snack, and for this dish they usually use sen lek, a 1/2-inch wide rice stick noodle.

SERVES 4

per serving
9.2g fat; 411 calories

serving suggestion
Although this dish is a complete meal in a bowl, the Thais usually accompany it with a soup such as tom yum goong (shrimp soup) which is consumed like a beverage throughout the meal.

 Remove seeds from the chiles if you prefer a milder flavor.

1 Place noodles in large heatproof bowl; cover with boiling water. Let stand until just tender; drain.

2 Heat wok or large non-stick skillet; stir-fry chicken, garlic, ginger and chile, in batches, until chicken is browned.

3 Return chicken mixture to wok with sugar, sauces and juice; stir-fry until sauce thickens slightly. Add noodles, scallions and sprouts to wok; stir-fry until hot. Serve phad thai sprinkled with cilantro.

chicken and potato stew

 preparation time 15 minutes • cooking time 30 minutes

1 1/2	tablespoons peanut oil
6	baby onions, quartered
2	cloves garlic, crushed
1 1/2	pounds boneless, skinless chicken thighs, chopped coarsely
10	ounces tiny new potatoes, quartered
2	large carrots, chopped coarsely
1/4	cup all-purpose flour
1/3	cup dry white wine
15	-ounce can chicken consomme
1	pound asparagus, trimmed, halved
3	tablespoons whole-grain mustard
1 1/2	tablespoons finely grated lemon peel
1/3	cup loosely packed, coarsely chopped fresh flat-leaf parsley

1 Heat oil in large non-stick pot; cook onions and garlic, stirring, until onions soften. Add chicken; cook, stirring, about 5 minutes or until chicken is browned and cooked through.

2 Add potatoes, carrots and flour; cook, stirring, 5 minutes. Add wine and consomme; cook, stirring, until mixture boils and thickens. Simmer, covered, about 10 minutes or until potatoes are tender.

3 Add asparagus, mustard and peel; bring to a boil. Reduce heat; simmer, covered, until asparagus is just tender. Stir in parsley.

SERVES 4

per serving 17.4g fat; 418 calories

serving suggestion Serve with a green salad.

 tip This recipe is more flavorsome if made a day ahead; store, covered, in refrigerator. Reheat just before serving.

spicy couscous chicken with fresh corn salsa

preparation time 15 minutes •
cooking time 12 minutes (plus let standing time)

1/2	teaspoon ground cumin
1/4	teaspoon ground coriander
1/4	teaspoon garam masala
1/4	teaspoon ground turmeric
1	cup chicken stock
1	cup couscous
1 1/2	pounds boneless, skinless chicken breasts
1	egg white, beaten lightly
2	ears fresh corn, shucked (about 1 pound)
2	medium tomatoes, seeded, chopped coarsely
1	small avocado, chopped coarsely
3	tablespoons red wine vinegar
4	scallions, chopped finely

Couscous, the North African cereal made from semolina, lends an intriguing crunch to the coating on the chicken.

1 Preheat oven to 425. Lightly oil large baking dish.

2 Cook spices in medium heated pot, stirring, until fragrant; add stock. Bring to a boil; stir in couscous. Remove from heat; let stand, covered, about 5 minutes or until stock is absorbed, fluffing with fork occasionally to separate grains.

3 Dip chicken in egg white; coat in couscous. Place chicken, in single layer, in prepared dish; bake, uncovered, about 10 minutes or until chicken is cooked through. Cover to keep warm.

4 Meanwhile, remove kernels from corn cobs. Cook kernels in small pot of boiling water, uncovered, about 2 minutes or until just tender; drain. Rinse under cold water; drain. Combine corn with remaining ingredients in medium bowl. Serve corn salsa with thickly sliced chicken.

SERVES 4

per serving
19.1g fat; 602 calories

serving suggestion
You might like to add some coarsely chopped fresh cilantro or finely chopped fresh chile to the corn salsa.

tip The salsa, without the avocado, can be prepared about 3 hours ahead; store, covered, in refrigerator. Add avocado just before serving.

chicken with lentil salsa

 preparation time 10 minutes • cooking time 15 minutes

2	teaspoons ground cumin
2	teaspoons ground coriander
1	teaspoon ground turmeric
12	chicken tenderloins (about 2 pounds)
1 1/2	cups red lentils
1	clove garlic, crushed
1	red serrano or Thai chile, seeded, chopped finely
1	small cucumber, seeded, chopped finely
1	medium red bell pepper, chopped finely
1/4	cup lemon juice
2	teaspoons peanut oil
3	tablespoons coarsely chopped fresh cilantro leaves
2	limes, cut into wedges

The spices of North Africa give the chicken a flavor-packed jolt in this dish. And, as it can be served hot or cold, this recipe is a good prepare-ahead dish.

SERVES 4

per serving
16.8g fat; 554 calories

serving suggestion
Serve accompanied with toasted pita bread or flour tortillas – or cracker bread, a large, flat, Middle Eastern bread – as the main course of a summer lunch.

1 Combine spices in medium bowl with chicken; toss to coat chicken with spices.

2 Cook lentils in large pot of boiling water, uncovered, until just tender; drain. Rinse under cold water; drain. Place lentils in large bowl with garlic, chile, cucumber, bell pepper, juice, oil and fresh cilantro.

3 Meanwhile, cook chicken on heated lightly oiled grill or grill pan until browned on both sides and cooked through. Add limes to pan; cook until browned on both sides. Serve chicken with lentil salsa and lime wedges.

chutney chicken breast with kashmiri pilaf

 preparation time 5 minutes • cooking time 25 minutes (plus let standing time)

1 1/2	tablespoons vegetable oil
1	small onion, chopped finely
1	clove garlic, crushed
1	teaspoon black or yellow mustard seeds
1/4	teaspoon ground cardamom
1/2	teaspoon ground cumin
1/2	teaspoon garam masala
1/2	teaspoon ground turmeric
1 1/2	cups long-grain white rice
3	cups chicken stock
3	tablespoons coarsely chopped fresh cilantro leaves
1/3	cup mango chutney
3	tablespoons water
4	boneless, skinless chicken breasts (1 1/2 pounds)

While many Indian dishes involve long, slow cooking, this recipe captures the essence of the cuisine in a quick and easy char-grill.

SERVES 4

per serving
15.3g fat; 613 calories

serving suggestion
Serve with some
extra mango chutney
and low-fat raita.

 tips Mango chutney will burn if the grill or pan is too hot. Black mustard seeds, which are more common than yellow in Indian cuisine, can be found in Asian markets or some health food stores.

1 Heat oil in medium pot; cook onion, garlic and mustard seeds, stirring, until onion softens and seeds pop. Add remaining spices; cook, stirring, until fragrant.

2 Add rice; stir to coat in spices. Add stock; bring to a boil. Reduce heat; simmer, uncovered, until rice is just tender. Stir in cilantro; keep warm.

3 Meanwhile, combine chutney with the water in small pot; cook, stirring, until heated through.

4 Cook chicken, brushing all over with chutney mixture, on heated oiled grill or grill pan until browned on both sides and cooked through. Cut into thick slices. Serve chutney chicken with pilaf.

thai fish cakes with noodle salad

 preparation time 15 minutes • cooking time 10 minutes

2/3	cup loosely packed fresh cilantro leaves
1/2	cup loosely packed fresh mint leaves
4	red serrano or Thai chiles, quartered
1 1/4	pounds firm white fish fillets, chopped coarsely
1	clove garlic, quartered
1	egg white, beaten lightly
8	ounces rice vermicelli
2	teaspoons sugar
1/4	cup lime juice
1 1/2	tablespoons Asian chili paste
1	small cucumber, seeded, chopped finely
3	ounces snow peas, sliced thinly

You can use practically any mild-flavored, skinless fish fillet in this recipe.

SERVES 4

per serving
5.1g fat; 375 calories

tip Fish cakes can be made in advance and frozen; defrost in refrigerator before cooking.

1 Blend or process half of the cilantro, half of the mint, half of the chile, fish, garlic and egg white until mixture forms a paste; shape into 12 patties.

2 Cook patties, in batches, in heated large non-stick skillet until browned on both sides and cooked through.

3 Meanwhile, place noodles in large heatproof bowl; cover with boiling water. Let stand until just tender; drain. Keep warm.

4 Combine sugar, juice and chili paste in small pot; bring to a boil. Reduce heat; simmer, stirring, until sugar dissolves.

5 Meanwhile, chop remaining cilantro, mint and chile finely. Place in large bowl with noodles, sugar mixture, cucumber and snow peas; toss to combine.

6 Serve fish cakes on noodle salad.

chicken scaloppini with gremolata

 preparation time 30 minutes • cooking time 30 minutes

2	large red bell peppers (about 1 1/4 pounds)
1/2	cup dry white wine
1/2	cup water
2	cups firmly packed, coarsely chopped fresh flat-leaf parsley
3	tablespoons coarsely grated lemon peel
3	tablespoons lemon juice
2	cloves garlic, quartered
8	boneless, skinless chicken breasts (3 pounds)
8	slices prosciutto (4 ounces)

Gremolata is to osso buco what cocktail sauce is to shrimp cocktail – you can't have one without the other. But this finely chopped blend of lemon peel, garlic and parsley is far too good to save for just the occasional veal shank or two... And it's very well-suited to chicken.

SERVES 8
per serving
10.7g fat; 287 calories

1 Quarter bell peppers; remove seeds and membranes. Roast under broiler, skin-side up, until skin blisters and blackens. Cover pepper pieces with plastic wrap or aluminum foil 5 minutes; peel away skin. Blend or process bell pepper, wine and the water until almost smooth; reserve.

2 Preheat oven to 350. Blend or process parsley, lemon peel, lemon juice and garlic until gremolata is almost smooth.

3 Cut chicken breasts in half horizontally almost all the way through; spread open each breast. Place between sheets of plastic wrap; pound gently with meat mallet. Divide gremolata among chicken breasts; roll each breast to enclose filling. Wrap each roll in prosciutto; secure with toothpicks.

4 Place chicken rolls in large, shallow greased baking dish; bake, uncovered, about 30 minutes or until chicken is cooked through.

5 Meanwhile, place bell pepper mixture in small pot; bring to a boil. Reduce heat; simmer, uncovered, about 3 minutes or until reduced by half. Add pan juices from chicken; return to a boil. Serve chicken on bell pepper sauce.

thai fish packages

 preparation time 10 minutes • cooking time 15 minutes

7	ounce rice stick noodles
4	5-ounce cod or snapper fillets
5	ounces baby bok choy, quartered
5	ounces snow peas, sliced thinly lengthwise
1	stalk fresh lemongrass, sliced thinly
1	rounded tablespoon grated lime peel
1	teaspoon soy sauce
3	tablespoons sweet Thai chili sauce
1	teaspoon fish sauce
3	tablespoons lime juice
1 1/2	tablespoons coarsely chopped fresh cilantro leaves

You can find lemongrass at Asian markets, or you can substitute grated lemon peel if you prefer.

1 Preheat oven to 425.

2 Place noodles in large heatproof bowl; cover with boiling water. Let stand until just tender; drain.

3 Divide noodles into four equal portions; place each on a large piece of aluminum foil. Top noodles with fish; top fish with equal amounts of bok choy, snow peas, lemongrass and peel. Drizzle with combined sauces and juice. Enclose fish stacks in foil; place in single layer on baking sheet.

4 Cook fish stacks 15 minutes or until fish is cooked through; open foil and transfer stacks to serving plates. Sprinkle with cilantro.

SERVES 4

per serving
4.4g fat; 333 calories

serving suggestion
Serve with wedges of lime or a salad made from fresh grapefruit or pummelo segments.

 tip Fish packages can be assembled several hours ahead; store in refrigerator.

pesto fish kebabs

 preparation time 10 minutes • cooking time 15 minutes

1 1/4	pounds firm white fish fillets
1 1/2	tablespoons bottled pesto
1/2	cup loosely packed, finely chopped, fresh flat-leaf parsley
1/2	small green cabbage (about 1 1/4 pounds), shredded finely
1/3	cup drained baby capers
1	teaspoon finely grated lemon peel
1/2	cup loosely packed, finely chopped fresh mint leaves

You can use any large fish fillets or steaks - such as cod, snapper, tuna or hake - for this recipe. Soak eight bamboo skewers in water at least 1 hour before using to avoid scorching and splintering.

1 Cut fish into 3/4-inch cubes; combine with pesto and 1 1/2 tablespoons of the parsley in medium bowl. Thread onto eight skewers.

2 Cook kebabs, in batches, in heated large lightly oiled skillet until browned and cooked as desired. Cover to keep warm.

3 Add cabbage to same heated skillet; cook, stirring, until just tender. Stir in remaining parsley, capers, lemon peel and mint.

4 Serve fish kebabs on stir-fried cabbage.

SERVES 4

per serving
5.2g fat; 194 calories

serving suggestion
Serve with lemon-scented steamed rice.

 tip Fish can be marinated and threaded onto skewers a day ahead; store, covered, in refrigerator.

fish and zucchini stacks on tomato salad

 preparation time 15 minutes • cooking time 10 minutes

4	7-ounce firm white fish fillets
2	medium green zucchini
2	medium yellow squash
4	medium tomatoes (about 1 3/4 pounds), sliced thinly
1/3	cup dry white wine coarsely ground black pepper
3	tablespoons balsamic vinegar
3	tablespoons baby basil leaves

You could use any firm, white-fleshed fish - cod, bream or snapper would be perfect for this recipe.

SERVES 4

per serving
5g fat; 263 calories

serving suggestion
Serve with a green salad and steamed potatoes.

tip Fish stacks can be assembled and wrapped in foil several hours ahead; store in refrigerator.

1 Preheat oven to 475.

2 Halve fish pieces lengthwise. Using vegetable peeler, peel zucchini into long thin ribbons.

3 Place four pieces of fish on large individual pieces of lightly oiled aluminum foil; top with zucchini ribbons then remaining fish pieces. Cut eight slices of tomato in half; place four half-slices on top of each stack. Drizzle stacks with wine; sprinkle with pepper.

4 Fold foil to enclose fish stacks; place in single layer in baking dish. Bake about 10 minutes or until fish is cooked through.

5 Divide remaining tomato slices equally among serving plates; top with unwrapped fish stacks. Drizzle stacks with vinegar; sprinkle with basil.

cheese-breaded fish fillets with stir-fried vegetables

preparation time 15 minutes • cooking time 15 minutes

1	cup stale whole-wheat breadcrumbs
1/2	cup rolled oats
1 1/2	tablespoons drained capers, chopped finely
2	teaspoons finely grated lemon peel
1/4	cup (1 ounce) freshly grated romano cheese
1/4	cup loosely packed, finely chopped fresh flat-leaf parsley
1 1/2	tablespoons sesame oil
4	5-ounce firm white fish fillets
1/2	cup flour
2	egg whites, beaten lightly
2	large carrots, sliced finely
2	trimmed celery stalks, sliced thinly
1	medium green bell pepper, sliced thinly
6	scallions, chopped finely
1	red serrano or Thai chile, seeded, chopped finely
1 1/2	tablespoons sesame seeds

You could use any firm-fleshed white fish fillets for this recipe - we used cod. Make the breadcrumbs from bread that is at least a day old; grate or process stale bread to make the crumbs.

SERVES 4

per serving
11.9g fat; 418 calories

serving suggestion
Serve with wedges
of lime or lemon.

 tip   Fish can be breaded several hours ahead; store, covered, in refrigerator.

1 Preheat oven to 425.

2 Combine breadcrumbs, oats, capers, lemon peel, cheese, parsley and oil in medium bowl. Coat fish in flour, shake off excess; dip in egg, then in breadcrumb mixture.

3 Place fish, in single layer, in baking dish; bake, uncovered, about 15 minutes or until cooked through.

4 Meanwhile, stir-fry carrots in heated large non-stick wok or skillet. Add celery, bell pepper, scallions, chile and sesame seeds; stir-fry until vegetables are just tender.

5 Serve sliced fish on stir-fried vegetables.

chicken, lentil and spinach pasta

 preparation time 10 minutes • cooking time 20 minutes

2	teaspoons vegetable oil
1	small onion, chopped finely
2	cloves garlic, crushed
5	ounces ground chicken
1/2	cup red lentils
2 3/4	cups chicken stock
3	tablespoons tomato paste
8	ounces baby spinach leaves
12	ounces shell pasta

1 Heat oil in medium skillet; cook onion and garlic, stirring, until onion softens. Add chicken; cook, stirring, until chicken has changed in color. Stir in lentils, stock and paste; simmer, uncovered, 10 minutes or until lentils are tender and sauce thickened. Add spinach; stir until spinach is just wilted.

2 Meanwhile, cook pasta in large pot of boiling salted water, uncovered, until just tender; drain.

3 Combine pasta and chicken mixture in large serving bowl.

SERVES 4

per serving 7.8g fat; 494 calories

tip This recipe is best made close to serving time.

vegetable tagine

preparation time 15 minutes • cooking time 15 minutes

1 1/2	tablespoons olive oil
1	medium onion, chopped coarsely
1	clove garlic, crushed
2	rounded tablespoons ground cumin
1 1/2	tablespoons ground coriander
2	teaspoons caraway seeds
2	medium eggplants (about 1 1/4 pounds), chopped
1	large zucchini, chopped
4	medium tomatoes (about 1 3/4 pounds), chopped
10 1/2	-ounce can garbanzos, drained, rinsed
1 1/2	tablespoons lemon juice
1	cup vegetable stock
1/3	cup chopped fresh cilantro leaves

A *tagine* is a delicious Moroccan stew, simmered and infused with the seasonings of North Africa.

SERVES 4

per serving 7.2g fat; 176 calories

tip This recipe can be made a day ahead; cover, refrigerate or freeze. Reheat and stir in cilantro just before serving.

1 Heat oil in large pot, add onion, garlic, spices, seeds and eggplant; cook, stirring, until onion is soft. Add zucchini, tomatoes and garbanzos; cook, stirring, about 5 minutes or until vegetables are just tender.

2 Stir in juice and stock; cook, uncovered, until mixture boils and thickens. Just before serving, stir in cilantro. Serve vegetable tagine with couscous, if desired.

SNACKS

These between-meal snacks will satisfy the heartiest of appetites – and your waist-line won't suffer for it. All of the recipes in this section call for pita bread; the pita you can find at Middle Eastern markets is often thicker than what can be bought at a regular grocery store. Any pita will do in these recipes – but the thicker, the better.

ham and asparagus grill

preparation time 10 minutes • cooking time 10 minutes

12	-ounce can asparagus, drained
1	large round pita bread
2	medium tomatoes, sliced
7	ounces lean shaved ham
3	tablespoons coarsely chopped fresh basil leaves
1	small red onion, sliced thinly
1	cup shredded low-fat mozzarella cheese

1. Place asparagus in small bowl; mash with fork until almost smooth.

2. Quarter bread; split pieces horizontally. Toast on both sides.

3. Divide remaining ingredients among the eight pieces of toast, finishing with cheese; cook under hot broiler until cheese melts.

SERVES 4
per serving 9.2g fat; 388 calories

salmon and tomato toasts

preparation time 10 minutes • cooking time 5 minutes

1 1/2	tablespoons drained capers, chopped finely
2	teaspoons finely chopped fresh dill tips
2	teaspoons olive oil
3	tablespoons lemon juice
1	large round pita bread
4	medium tomatoes (about 1 3/4 pounds), seeded, sliced thinly
4	green onions, sliced thinly
8	ounces smoked salmon

1. Combine capers, dill, oil and juice in small bowl.

2. Quarter bread; split pieces horizontally. Toast on both sides.

3. Divide combined tomato and onion among the eight pieces of toast; top with salmon. Drizzle with caper mixture.

SERVES 4
per serving 4.5g fat; 315 calories

vegetable grill

preparation time 25 minutes (plus standing time) • cooking time 30 minutes

6	large carrots (about 1 pound), chopped coarsely
1/4	cup buttermilk
2	teaspoons ground cumin
2	teaspoons ground coriander
2	large red bell peppers (about 1 1/2 pounds)
4	baby eggplants, sliced thinly
1	large red onion, sliced thickly
6	ounces mushrooms, sliced thickly
14	-ounce can artichoke hearts, drained, chopped coarsely
1	large round pita bread
1	cup (4 ounces) shredded low-fat cheddar cheese

1. Boil, steam or microwave carrots until just tender; drain. Blend or process carrots with buttermilk until smooth.

2. Cook spices in small dry heated skillet until fragrant. Combine with carrot mixture; cover to keep warm.

3. Quarter bell peppers; remove seeds and membranes. Roast under broiler, skin-side up, until skin blisters and blackens; cover peppers with plastic or aluminum foil for 5 minutes. Peel away skin; slice peppers thickly.

4. Cook eggplants, onion, mushrooms and artichokes, in batches, on heated oiled grill or grill pan until browned and just tender.

5. Quarter bread, split pieces horizontally; toast on both sides.

6. Divide carrot mixture equally among the eight pieces of toast; top with peppers, eggplant, mushrooms and artichoke. Sprinkle cheese equally over pieces; cook under hot broiler until cheese melts.

SERVES 4

per serving 6.4g fat; 422 calories

We're wheeling out a luscious-looking dessert cart in this chapter, one groaning with such delicious time- and waist-saving recipes that you'll have no problem fulfilling your friends' and family's craving for a happy ending.

satsuma plum clafouti

 preparation time 15 minutes • cooking time 40 minutes

1 1/2	cups low-fat prepared custard or vanilla pudding
1/4	cup self-rising flour
1	egg yolk
2	egg whites
28	-ounce can whole plums, drained, halved, pitted
2	teaspoons powdered sugar

The large plums that are most frequently used in canned fruits, sometimes called Indian blood plums, have a distinctive, dark-red to purple fibrous flesh. They're extremely juicy and pleasantly sweet.

SERVES 4

per serving 2.6g fat; 244 calories

serving suggestion Serve with a scoop of low-fat ice-cream.

 tip   Canned apricots or peaches can be substituted for plums.

1 Preheat oven to 350.

2 Combine custard, flour and egg yolk in medium bowl.

3 Beat egg whites in small bowl with an electric mixer until soft peaks form; fold gently into custard mixture. Pour into 9- to 10-inch pie plate.

4 Pat plums dry with paper towels; arrange plums, cut-side down, over custard. Place pie plate on baking sheet. Bake, uncovered, about 40 minutes or until firm.

5 Just before serving, dust with sifted powdered sugar.

rice pudding with rhubarb and raspberries

 preparation time 10 minutes • cooking time 1 hour

4	cups skim milk
2/3	cup sugar
1/2	cup arborio or other short-grained rice
1	pound rhubarb, trimmed, chopped coarsely
1/4	cup sugar
7	ounces raspberries

The Greeks invented the partnership of rice and milk for dessert. They call it rizógalo; we call it seriously good comfort food.

1 Combine milk and 2/3 cup sugar in medium pot; bring to a boil. Stir in rice; reduce heat. Simmer, covered, about 1 hour or until rice is creamy, stirring occasionally with wooden spoon.

2 Meanwhile, combine rhubarb and extra 1/4 cup sugar in large pot. Cook over low heat, stirring, about 10 minutes or until rhubarb is tender.

3 Layer rice pudding and rhubarb mixture in serving dishes, finishing with rhubarb; sprinkle with raspberries.

SERVES 4

per serving
0.7g fat; 443 calories

 tips — Any berry – boysenberries, blackberries, strawberries – can be substituted for the raspberries.
A pinch of grated nutmeg or ground cardamom can be added to the rice mixture.

mocha self-saucing pudding

 preparation time 10 minutes • cooking time 45 minutes

1	cup self-rising flour
1/3	cup cocoa powder
3/4	cup sugar
2 1/2	teaspoons instant coffee
1/2	cup skim milk
1 1/2	tablespoons vegetable oil
1/2	cup firmly packed brown sugar
1 1/4	cups boiling water
1 1/2	tablespoons powdered sugar

1 Preheat oven to 325.

2 Sift flour, 3 tablespoons of the cocoa, sugar and 2 teaspoons of the coffee into a 5-cup baking dish; gradually stir in milk and oil.

3 Sift brown sugar, remaining cocoa and remaining coffee evenly over flour mixture; gently pour the water over brown sugar mixture. Bake pudding, uncovered, about 45 minutes; serve dusted with sifted powdered sugar.

SERVES 4

per serving 6.3g fat; 496 calories

serving suggestion
Raspberries or blueberries with whipped cream make a good accompaniment.

Originally the name of a Middle-Eastern seaport from which premium Arabic coffee was exported, the word mocha has evolved to describe the serendipitous combination of coffee and chocolate.

 tip This pudding is best served hot, because the sauce is quickly absorbed by the pudding.

peach galette

 preparation time 10 minutes • cooking time 15 minutes

1/2   sheet ready-rolled puff pastry, thawed

3   medium peaches (about 1 pound)

1 1/2   tablespoons brown sugar

1 1/2   tablespoons apricot or raspberry preserves, warmed

A galette is a French, flaky-pastry tart that can be either savory or sweet, and it makes a popular summer dessert. Seasonal fruits such as plums or nectarines can be substituted for the peaches.

SERVES 6

per serving
6.4g fat; 144 calories

serving suggestion
serve sprinkled with
powdered sugar.

1 Preheat oven to 425. Place pastry on lightly greased baking sheet.

2 Place unpeeled peaches in large heatproof bowl; cover with boiling water. Let stand about 1 minute or until skins can be slipped off peaches easily. Slice peaches thinly; discard pits.

3 Arrange peach slices on pastry, leaving 3/4-inch border around edge; fold over edges of pastry. Sprinkle sugar evenly over peach galette.

4 Bake galette about 15 minutes or until pastry is browned lightly. Brush hot galette with preserves.

lemon cakes with passion fruit syrup

 preparation time 10 minutes • cooking time 25 minutes

1 1/4	cups self-rising flour
1/2	cup sugar
2	teaspoons finely grated lemon peel
1	egg, beaten lightly
3	tablespoons butter, melted
3	tablespoons skim milk
3/4	cup low-fat yogurt
1	cup water
1	teaspoon cornstarch
1/2	cup passion fruit pulp or crushed pineapple
3	tablespoons finely sliced lemon peel

SERVES 8

per serving
5.1g fat; 197 calories

serving suggestion
You could scatter a few berries, such as blueberries or raspberries, on each serving plate.

tip Lime peel can be substituted for lemon peel.

You will need about six passion fruit to make this recipe. The thin-skinned purple-black variety will yield much more pulp than the thicker-skinned yellow-fleshed fruit.

1 Preheat oven to 350. Grease eight holes of a 12-hole muffin pan.

2 Combine flour in medium bowl with 1/4 cup of the sugar and grated peel. Add egg, butter, milk and yogurt; stir until just combined. Divide mixture among prepared pan holes; bake about 25 minutes. Let cakes cool in pan 5 minutes; turn out onto wire rack.

3 Meanwhile, combine the water and remaining sugar in small pot. Stir over medium heat until sugar dissolves; bring to a boil. Reduce heat; simmer, uncovered, without stirring, 10 minutes. Stir in blended cornstarch and passion fruit until mixture boils and thickens. Strain into small heatproof measuring cup; discard seeds. Stir in sliced peel; cool.

4 Serve lemon cakes with passion fruit syrup.

pineapple crunch

 preparation time 10 minutes • cooking time 20 minutes

28	-ounce can crushed pineapple, drained
2	small Asian pears, chopped coarsely
1 1/2	tablespoons Malibu liqueur
3	cups wheat-flake fruit-and-nuts cereal
3	tablespoons pumpkin seeds
3	tablespoons sunflower seeds
1/3	cup low-fat yogurt
3	tablespoons honey

We used Just Right breakfast cereal in this recipe but you can use any wheat-flakes and dried-fruit cereal, even a muesli or granola-like product.

1 Preheat oven to 350. Grease four 1-cup ovenproof custard cups or ramekins; place on baking pan.

2 Combine pineapple, pears and Malibu in medium bowl; divide among prepared dishes.

3 Crumble cereal by hand in same bowl; stir in seeds, yogurt and honey. Divide mixture among prepared dishes; bake, uncovered, about 20 minutes or until browned lightly.

SERVES 4

per serving 8g fat; 410 calories

serving suggestion Serve topped with low-fat yogurt or low-fat ice-cream and a dollop of fresh pureed mango, passion fruit pulp or drizzle of honey.

 tip You can substitute chopped and drained canned peaches or apricots for the pineapple in this recipe.

ricotta and berry trifle

 preparation time 15 minutes

7	ounces raspberries
7	ounces blueberries
7	ounces strawberries, quartered
2	cups low-fat ricotta cheese
1/3	cup orange juice
1/3	cup maple syrup
1	ounce crumbled meringue cookies
1 1/2	tablespoons toasted sliced almonds

The traditional English favorite is given a new look with this summery update. If you prefer, the trifle can be served in a large glass bowl. Meringue cookies are sometimes called divinity or kisses.

1 Combine berries in medium bowl.

2 Blend or process cheese, juice and maple syrup until smooth.

3 Divide a quarter of the cheese mixture among four 1-cup dessert glasses; sprinkle with some of the berries. Repeat layering with remaining cheese mixture and berries, finishing with berries.

4 Sprinkle meringue and nuts over trifles. Cover; refrigerate 3 hours.

SERVES 4

per serving
11g fat; 293 calories

serving suggestion
You can drizzle some pureed berries over the top of the trifles.

apple and fig bread pudding

 preparation time 20 minutes • cooking time 50 minutes

3	tablespoons honey
3	tablespoons water
8	slices thick white bread
1	medium apple, cored, quartered, sliced thinly
12	dried figs, halved
2	cups skim milk
2	eggs
3	tablespoons sugar
1/2	teaspoon ground cinnamon
2	teaspoons powdered sugar

Granny Smith and golden delicious are the best apple varieties to use for this recipe.

SERVES 4

per serving
3g fat; 283 calories

serving suggestion
A dollop of low-fat yogurt, swirled with honey and cinnamon, or some fresh raspberries makes a good accompaniment.

tip Remove bread and butter pudding from water bath immediately after cooking to prevent it from overcooking and becoming tough.

1 Preheat oven to 325. Lightly grease 5-cup baking dish.

2 Stir honey and the water in small pot over low heat until honey melts.

3 Cut crusts from bread; discard crusts. Halve slices diagonally; brush both sides of bread with honey mixture. Layer bread, apple and figs, overlapping pieces slightly.

4 Whisk milk, eggs and sugar together in medium bowl; strain into large measuring cup, skimming and discarding any foam. Pour half the milk mixture over the bread; let stand 5 minutes. Pour over remaining milk mixture; sprinkle with cinnamon.

5 Place dish in larger baking dish; add enough boiling water to come halfway up sides of dish. Bake pudding, uncovered, about 45 minutes or until top is browned lightly and pudding is set. Dust with sifted powdered sugar before serving.

chocolate mousse

 preparation time 5 minutes (plus refrigeration time)

2	teaspoons instant coffee
1	teaspoon hot water
4	ounces dark chocolate, melted
14	ounces low-fat French vanilla yogurt
1 1/2	tablespoons Irish cream liqueur

We used Baileys Original Irish Cream, based on Irish whiskey, spirits and cream, in this recipe.

1 Combine coffee and the water in medium bowl, stirring until coffee dissolves. Add chocolate, yogurt and liqueur, stirring, until combined.

2 Divide among four small (3/4-cup) serving dishes. Cover; refrigerate about 30 minutes or until firm.

SERVES 4

per serving 9.1g fat; 256 calories

serving suggestion
Raspberries, strawberries or blueberries are an appealing accompaniment to this mousse.

tip Mousse can be prepared a day ahead; store, covered, in refrigerator until just before serving.

caramelized oranges with ice-cream

 preparation time 10 minutes • cooking time 10 minutes

4	large oranges (about 2 1/2 pounds)
3	tablespoons brown sugar
3	tablespoons Grand Marnier
7	ounces low-fat vanilla ice-cream

Navel oranges are ideal for this recipe because they have very few seeds.

1 Peel oranges, removing as much white pith as possible; cut crosswise into thick slices.

2 Place oranges, in single layer, on baking pan. Sprinkle with sugar; drizzle with liqueur. Cook oranges on both sides under hot broiler until just caramelized.

3 Divide ice-cream and oranges among four serving dishes; drizzle with pan juices.

SERVES 4

per serving 3.2g fat; 215 calories

serving suggestion
Sprinkle some finely chopped mint or purple basil over the oranges.

tip Cointreau or Triple Sec can be substituted for Grand Marnier.

guilt-free tiramisu

 preparation time 20 minutes (plus refrigeration time)

1 1/2	tablespoons instant coffee
3/4	cup boiling water
3	tablespoons marsala
4	-ounce package ladyfingers
1	cup low-fat ricotta
1/2	cup light sour cream
3	tablespoons sugar
3	teaspoons cocoa powder

Tiramisu, translated roughly as "pick-me-up," is usually made of savoiardi (ladyfingers) soaked in coffee and marsala, layered with tons of mascarpone and topped with cream. Our version is no less delicious... But far, far less laden with fat!

SERVES 6

per serving
7.8g fat; 181 calories

serving suggestion
stirring about 1/2 cup pureed fresh strawberries or mango into the ricotta mixture is a nice addition to this dessert ... and, of course, accompany it with tiny cups of good espresso.

1 Dissolve coffee in the boiling water in medium bowl; stir in marsala. Set aside 18 ladyfingers; coarsely chop remaining cookies.

2 Position three ladyfingers upright in each of six 3/4-cup glasses; drizzle with half of the coffee mixture.

3 Beat ricotta, sour cream and sugar with electric mixer in small bowl for about 4 minutes or until mixture just thickens slightly. Divide half of the ricotta mixture among glasses; sprinkle with chopped ladyfingers. Drizzle with remaining coffee mixture; top with remaining ricotta mixture.

4 Dust each tiramisu with sifted cocoa. Cover; refrigerate 3 hours or overnight before serving.

apple and cinnamon pancakes with maple syrup

 preparation time 20 minutes · cooking time 20 minutes

1	cup self-rising flour
1/4	cup firmly packed brown sugar
1/2	teaspoon ground cinnamon
1/2	cup skim milk
1	egg yolk
1/2	cup canned apple-pie filling, chopped coarsely
2	egg whites
2	Granny Smith apples, peeled, cored, cut into wedges
3	tablespoons brown sugar
7	ounces low-fat vanilla ice-cream
3	tablespoons maple syrup

Maple syrup, the processed sap of the maple tree, has a natural affinity with apple. Don't use maple-flavored syrup or pancake syrup, which is made from cane sugar and artificial maple flavoring - it's not a good substitute.

SERVES 4

per serving
2.1g fat; 277 calories

serving suggestion
A flavored ice-cream, such as toffee crunch or butterscotch, can be used instead of vanilla; omit the maple syrup if you use a flavored ice-cream.

1 Combine flour in large bowl with 1/4 cup sugar, cinnamon, milk, egg yolk and pie filling.

2 Beat egg whites in small bowl with electric mixer until soft peaks form; fold gently into apple mixture.

3 Heat medium non-stick skillet; pour in 1/4-cup amounts of batter for each pancake. Cook until browned on both sides; repeat with remaining batter to make eight pancakes.

4 Cook apple wedges and 3 tablespoons sugar over low heat in same pan, stirring, until apple caramelizes.

5 Divide pancakes among serving dishes. Top with apple mixture, then ice-cream; drizzle with maple syrup.

GLOSSARY

almond
BLANCHED skins removed.
GROUND also known as almond meal.
MEAL also known as finely ground almonds; powdered to a flour-like texture.
SLICED paper-thin slices.
SLIVERED small length-wise-cut pieces.

baking powder a rising agent consisting mainly of two parts cream of tartar to one part bicarbonate of soda (baking soda).

barley flakes flattened grains produced by steaming the barley grain then rolling it into flakes.

bok choy also called pak choi or Chinese white cabbage; has a fresh, mild mustard taste. Baby bok choy is also widely available.

breadcrumbs
PACKAGED fine-textured, crunchy, purchased, white breadcrumbs.
STALE one- or two-day-old bread made into crumbs by grating, blending or processing.

bulghur hulled and steamed wheat kernels that are dried and crushed.

celeriac root vegetable with brown skin, white flesh and a celery-like flavor.

cheese
CHEDDAR a semi-hard cow-milk cheese; we used a low-fat variety with a fat content of not more than 7%.
CREAM mild-flavored fresh cheese made of cow milk; we used one with 21% fat.
FETA salty white cheese made from cow milk, though sheep- and goat-milk varieties are available. We used low-fat feta with 15% fat content.
MOZZARELLA soft, spun-curd cheese traditionally made from water buffalo milk; cow-milk versions of this product, sometimes called pizza cheese, are available. We used a version with 17.5% fat.
PARMESAN also known as parmigiano, parmesan is a hard, grainy cow-milk cheese which originated in Italy. Parmigiano reggiano is generally aged longer than grana padano.
RICOTTA a low-fat, fresh unripened cheese made from whey with 8.5% fat.
ROMANO hard sheep- or cow-milk cheese; straw-colored and grainy in texture.

chiles available in many different types and sizes. Use rubber gloves when chopping and seeding fresh chiles as they can burn your skin. Removing seeds lessens the heat level.

chinese broccoli also known as gai lum.

chinese cabbage also known as Peking cabbage or wong bok.

coconut milk we used a canned light coconut milk with a fat content of less than 6%.

cooking-oil spray we used a cholesterol-free cooking spray made from canola oil.

cornstarch used as a thickening agent in cooking.

cornmeal ground dried corn; available in different textures.

couscous a fine, grain-like cereal product, made from semolina.

curry paste
MASALA literally meaning blended spices; a masala can be whole spices, a paste or a powder, and can include herbs as well as spices and other seasonings. Traditional dishes are usually named after particular masalas.
TANDOORI consists of garlic, tamarind, ginger, coriander, chile, spices and sometimes red food coloring.

five-spice powder a fragrant mixture of ground cinnamon, cloves, star anise, Sichuan pepper and fennel seeds.

flour
BUCKWHEAT although not a true cereal, flour is made from its seeds. It's available from health food stores, if not in your local supermarket.
SELF-RISING all-purpose flour combined with baking powder in the proportion of 1 cup flour to 2 teaspoons baking powder.

garam masala a blend of spices, originating in North India; based on varying proportions of cardamom, cinnamon, cloves, coriander, fennel and cumin, roasted and ground together.

garbanzos also called chickpeas, hummus or channa; an irregularly round, sandy-colored legume.

ginger, fresh also known as green or root ginger; the thick gnarled root of a tropical plant. Can be kept, peeled, covered with dry sherry in a jar and refrigerated, or frozen in an airtight container.

grand marnier orange-flavored liqueur.

ham we used lean ham which has a fat content of approximately 4% – about half that of regular leg ham.

indian bread naan, chapatti, roti and pappadums are all varieties of indian breads. They are available in specialty food stores, Asian markets and in the international food section of some supermarkets.

irish cream we used Baileys Original Irish Cream, based on Irish whiskey, spirits and cream.

lamb
FILLET tenderloin; the smaller piece of meat from a row of loin chops or rib chops.
RIB CHOPS small, tender cutlet.

lamington pan a 8- x 12-inch sheet-cake pan that is 1 1/4 inches deep.

lemongrass a tall, clumping, lemon-smelling and -tasting, sharp-edged grass; the white lower part of each stem is chopped and used in Asian cooking. Don't buy it dried; fresh is best, and frozen will do in a pinch. You can also substitute the zest (grated peel) of one lemon for two stalks of lemongrass.

lentils dried pulses often identified by and named after their color; also known as dhal.

low-fat custard we used trim custard with 0.9% fat.

low-fat ice cream we used an ice-cream with 3% fat.

low-fat mayonnaise we used cholesterol-free mayonnaise with 3% fat.

low-fat sour cream we used light sour cream with 18.5% fat.

low-fat whipped cream we used whipped cream with 18% fat.

low-fat yogurt we used yogurt with a fat content of less than 0.2%.

malibu
coconut-flavored rum.

maple syrup
distilled sap of the maple tree. Maple-flavored syrup or pancake syrup is made from cane sugar and artificial maple flavoring and is not an adequate substitute for the real thing.

mesclun mixed baby salad leaves also sold as salad mix or gourmet salad mix; a mixture of assorted young lettuce and other green leaves.

mushrooms
BUTTON small, cultivated white mushrooms having a delicate, subtle flavor.

CREMINI light to dark brown mushrooms with full-bodied flavor. Button or cup mushrooms can be substituted for cremini mushrooms.
OYSTER gray-white fan-shaped mushroom.

noodles
ASIAN also known as hokkein or stir-fry noodles; fresh egg noodles resembling thick, yellow-brown spaghetti needing no pre-cooking before being used.
FRESH RICE thick, wide, almost white in color; made from rice and vegetable oil. Must be covered with boiling water to remove starch and excess oil before using in soups and stir-fries.
RICE STICK a dried noodle, available flat and wide or very thin; made from rice flour and water.

parsley, flat-leaf also known as continental parsley or Italian parsley.

passion fruit a small tropical fruit, native to Brazil, comprised of a tough outer skin surrounding edible black sweet-sour seeds.

polenta cereal made of ground corn; also the name of the dish made from it.

rhubarb a vegetable; only the firm, reddish stems are eaten.

rice
ARBORIO small, round grain rice well-suited to absorb a large amount of liquid.
BASMATI RICE a white fragrant long-grain rice.
BROWN natural whole grain.
JASMINE fragrant long-grained rice.
LONG-GRAIN elongated grain, remains separate when cooked.
WILD blackish brown seed from North America is not a member of the rice family. It is fairly expensive as it's difficult to cultivate but has a delicious nutty flavor.

rice flakes available from supermarkets and health food stores; also known as parva in India.

rice paper sheets mostly from Vietnam (banh trang). Made from rice paste and stamped into rounds, with a woven pattern. Store well at room temperature, but are quite brittle and will break if dropped. Dipped in water, they become pliable wrappers for fried food and for eating fresh (uncooked) vegetables.

rye flakes flat flakes of crushed rye grain.

sauces
FISH made from salted pulverized fermented fish, usually anchovies. Has strong taste and pungent smell.
HOISIN SAUCE a thick, sweet and spicy Chinese paste made from salted fermented soy beans, onions and garlic; used as a marinade or baste, or to accent stir-fries and barbecued or roasted foods.
KETJAP MANIS Indonesian sweet, thick soy sauce which has sugar and spices added. You can also make your own substitute by combining equal parts soy sauce and molasses or brown sugar, then boiling the mixture until the sugar dissolves.
OYSTER Asian in origin, this sauce is made from oysters and their brine, cooked with salt and soy sauce, and thickened with starches.
SATAY traditional Indonesian/Malaysian spicy peanut sauce served with grilled meat skewers.
SOY made from fermented soy beans; several varieties are available in supermarkets and Asian food stores.

SWEET THAI CHILI a comparatively mild sauce made from red chiles, sugar, garlic and vinegar.

TABASCO brand name of an extremely fiery sauce made from vinegar, hot red peppers and salt.

TERIYAKI a homemade or commercially bottled sauce usually made from soy sauce, mirin, sugar, ginger and other spices; it imparts a distinctive glaze when brushed on meat to be grilled.

TOMATO PASTA SAUCE, BOTTLED prepared sauce available from supermarkets; sometimes labeled sugo.

sesame
OIL made from roasted, crushed, white sesame seeds; a flavoring rather than a cooking medium.
SEEDS black and white are the most common of the oval seeds harvested from the tropical plant *Sesamum indicum*; however there are red and brown varieties also. Used in za'atar, halva and tahini and a good source of calcium. To toast, spread seeds evenly on oven tray, toast in moderate oven briefly.

soy whole-grain flakes calcium-rich flakes made from soy beans.

sugar
we used coarse granulated table sugar unless otherwise specified.
BROWN a soft, fine sugar retaining molasses.
POWDERED also known as confectioners' sugar.
RAW natural brown granulated sugar.

sunflower seeds kernels from dried husked sunflower seeds.

tofu also known as bean curd, an off-white, custard-like product made from the milk of crushed soy beans; comes fresh as soft or firm, and processed as fried or pressed dried sheets. Leftover fresh tofu can be refrigerated in water (which is changed daily) up to 4 days. Silken tofu refers to the method by which it is made – where it is strained through silk.

tortilla unleavened bread sold frozen, fresh or vacuum-packed; made from wheat flour or corn.

triticale a nutritious hybrid of wheat (triticum) and rye (secale) which contains more protein and less gluten than wheat and has nutty sweet flavor. Available in whole grain, flour and flakes.

unprocessed bran made from the outer layer of a cereal, usually the husks of wheat, rice or oats.

vinegar
BALSAMIC authentic only from the province of Modena, Italy; made from a regional wine of white Trebbiano grapes specially processed then aged in antique wooden casks to give the exquisite pungent flavor.
RED WINE based on fermented red wine.
WHITE made from spirit of cane sugar.
WHITE WINE made from white wine.

wheat germ small creamy flakes milled from the embryo of the wheat.

MAKE YOUR OWN STOCK

These recipes can be made up to 4 days ahead and stored, covered, in the refrigerator. Be sure to remove any fat from the surface after the cooled stock has been refrigerated overnight. If the stock is to be kept longer, it is best to freeze it in smaller quantities.

Stock is also available in cans or tetra packs. Stock cubes or powder can be used. As a guide, 1 teaspoon of stock powder or 1 small crumbled stock cube mixed with 1 cup water will give a fairly strong stock. Be aware of the salt and fat content of stock cubes and powders and prepared stocks.

All stock recipes make about 10 cups.

beef stock

4	pounds meaty beef bones
2	medium onions
2	sticks celery, chopped
2	medium carrots, chopped
3	bay leaves
2	teaspoons black peppercorns
20	cups water
12	cups water, extra

Place bones and unpeeled chopped onions in baking dish. Bake in hot oven about 1 hour or until bones and onions are well browned. Transfer bones and onions to large pan, add celery, carrots, bay leaves, peppercorns and water, simmer, uncovered, 3 hours. Add extra water, simmer, uncovered, further 1 hour; strain.

chicken stock

4	pounds chicken bones
2	medium onions, chopped
2	sticks celery, chopped
2	medium carrots, chopped
3	bay leaves
2	teaspoons black peppercorns
20	cups water

Combine all ingredients in large pan, simmer, uncovered, 2 hours; strain.

fish stock

3	pounds fish bones
12	cups water
1	medium onion, chopped
2	stick celery, chopped
2	bay leaves
1	teaspoon black peppercorns

Combine all ingredients in large pan, simmer, uncovered, 20 minutes; strain.

vegetable stock

2	large carrots, chopped
2	large parsnips, chopped
4	medium onions, chopped
12	sticks celery, chopped
4	bay leaves
2	teaspoons black peppercorns
24	cups water

Combine all ingredients in large pan, simmer, uncovered, 1 1/2 hours; strain.